50

ENGAGING
MONITORING
FOCUSING
BUILDING
TEACHING

STRATEGIES
FOR YOUR VIRTUAL
CLASSROOM

Jennifer Jump, M.A.

Contributing Authors

Saskia Lacey

Kiley E. Smith

Publishing Credits

Corinne Burton, M.A.Ed., *Publisher*

Aubrie Nielsen, M.S.Ed., *Exec. VP of Content Development*

Emily Smith, M.A.Ed., *VP of Content Development*

Véronique Bos, *Creative Director*

Robin Erickson, *Art Director*

Dani Neiley, *Associate Content Specialist*

Image Credits

Screen captures Teacher Created Materials; all other images iStock and/or Shutterstock

Shell Education

A division of Teacher Created Materials

5482 Argosy Avenue

Huntington Beach, CA 92649-1039

www.tcmpub.com/shell-education

ISBN 978-1-0876-4228-4

© 2021 Shell Educational Publishing, Inc.

Table of Contents

Welcome

Virtual teaching is not new, but a complete reliance on educating students in virtual classrooms is. There were few distance-learning experts in March 2020, when COVID-19 forced students and teachers around the world into virtual learning environments. As educators, our heads were spinning with definitions of new instructional strategies, such as synchronous and asynchronous learning. Our brick-and-mortar classrooms have always been crucial environments for building relationships with students, supporting their academic growth, engaging with rich texts, solving complex problems, and answering difficult questions. Seminars, turn-and-talks, gallery walks—these teaching strategies made our classrooms collaborative and inclusive. As the spring of 2020 passed, educational systems strengthened and defined new and innovative ways to support students.

This book is born from the work of courageous educators around the world who began innovating in the face of unprecedented challenges. Working with teachers, I began diving into ways to engage with students virtually. Honest and vulnerable conversations opened doors to connections with students through their monitors. I led virtual "coffee chats" with hundreds of educators, building community with them and collaborating around ideas that would form the base of this collection of strategies. This collection is not exhaustive, as we are evolving constantly to best meet the ever-changing needs of our students, our classrooms, and our schools.

Nothing about this transition has been easy, but together, we—the educational force—are finding our way. We have tried new strategies, learned how excruciating wait time can feel via video, struggled with online whiteboard platforms, researched websites and apps well into our Saturday evenings, and scrutinized our recorded instruction with critical eyes. All this is helping us to develop our expertise in the world of distance learning.

Make the strategies in this resource your own and inspire the students in your virtual classroom, just as you always have when you were in the room with them. Keep the love of learning alive for yourself and your students. Good teaching is good teaching—no matter the learning environment.

~Jen Jump

Tips for Distance-Learning Environments

Each district and school outlines parameters for distance learning. Within those guidelines, plan both synchronous and asynchronous lessons for your students, as well as activities for independent learning. Hold some synchronous meetings for the whole class, but also plan sessions with smaller groups of students or individuals to meet their specific learning needs.

It is imperative to identify the specific components of instruction that work best for synchronous or asynchronous instruction. When planning, consider the touch points for instruction, the modeling students need, and the supports that will scaffold instruction.

Consider the following questions when planning distance learning:

- What are the objectives for this lesson?
- What background information do my students have?
- How will students engage with new vocabulary words?
- How will I use formative assessment?
- What needs to be modeled for students?
- During which parts of the lesson will students need guided practice?
- How will I know when students have mastered the objectives?
- What instruction will be offered if students need additional support?

Synchronous Instruction

Synchronous instruction happens in real time. The teacher and students are in the virtual classroom together, learning, listening, and discussing in virtual lessons. For successful synchronous learning, prepare for virtual instruction before class meetings begin—just as you would in a brick-and-mortar classroom. Have your materials ready, which includes cued up web pages or videos that support instruction.

Ensure all students have a clear understanding of the virtual classroom expectations, including the use of cameras, when to mute and unmute, how and when to use chat features, and how to demonstrate engagement. Practicing these expectations will maximize student participation and minimize distractions during instruction.

Keep using the tools that work in classrooms. For example, during live video lessons, use chart paper for brainstorming, building background information, creating anchor charts, or documenting students' responses. Or, have students do their work in printed student books and take pictures of their completed pages to email to you.

Develop a routine for synchronous instruction. Knowing what to expect when they enter the virtual classroom allows students to feel confident and prepared. When a routine is in place, students are able to focus on the instructional content and learning opportunities, rather than feel distracted or insecure about what might happen during class.

Clearly articulate the goals and purposes of each synchronous lesson. Student-friendly and standards-based language will support rigorous lesson objectives while ensuring students can communicate the purpose of the lesson.

Keep synchronous sessions succinct, and don't plan too many activities for each session. Activities take longer in a virtual environment than they might in a physical classroom. If possible, use breakout rooms within an online meeting platform to allow students to share ideas in small groups during live virtual lessons. Then, plan time for the whole group to come together and debrief learning through shared screens.

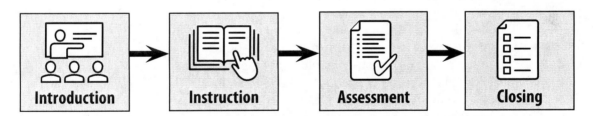

| **Introduction** | **Instruction** | **Assessment** | **Closing** |

A consistent introduction helps create classroom community and builds relationships within the classroom. As soon as students enter the classroom, they should find themselves engaged in learning with a clear understanding of the materials they need to be successful.

Plan instruction that meets the needs of your students and the specific learning objectives for a lesson. Consider using the *gradual release of responsibility* model of instruction. This model follows an "I Do" (teacher modeling), "We Do" (guided practice), "You Do" (independent practice) model of instruction. In a virtual setting, synchronous class meetings are often used for the "I Do" and "We Do" parts of a lesson.

Tips for Distance-Learning Environments (cont.)

Synchronous Instruction (cont.)

Introduction

(cont.)

Another instructional model that works well in virtual settings is a *flipped classroom*. This approach uses synchronous class time for practice activities or discussions, while asynchronous or independent time is used to provide direct instruction via recorded videos. Each of these models has value in synchronous learning, depending on the goals of the lesson.

During synchronous learning, consider all learners as you plan for engagement within the lesson. Use a variety of strategies to provide all students ample opportunities to engage in comfortable and familiar ways. And, incorporate best practices around culturally responsive learning and social-emotional learning (see pages 13–14).

Providing students with adequate think time can be particularly challenging in a virtual environment. Be sure to include wait time in planned lessons, and make a conscious effort to practice it while delivering instruction.

Assessment

Use formative assessment to gain valuable information about students' responses to instruction. Formative assessment allows students to demonstrate their understanding of a lesson or a concept. Virtual formative assessment can be done through polls, quizzes, observations, exit tickets, and written responses. Apps such as Kahoot! and Quizizz allow students to participate in a game while providing the teacher with opportunities for informal assessment. Have students write answers in their books, on sheets of paper, or on sticky notes. Then, they can hold their written responses up to their cameras for quick assessment opportunities. Use information from formative assessments to determine small groups for reteaching, acceleration, or other support.

Closing

A consistent lesson closing and summary of next steps provides students with clear expectations for independent learning following synchronous instruction. Be sure to provide step-by-step assignments in writing (including pictures when appropriate) and orally.

Asynchronous Instruction

Asynchronous instruction does not happen in real time; it often includes brief, prerecorded direct instruction by the teacher. Providing direct instruction asynchronously fits the flipped classroom model. Recorded lessons offer students the opportunity to pause, rewind, and rewatch instruction to increase their understanding. Recorded lessons can be shared via a school's learning management system or other online platforms.

As with synchronous instruction, asynchronous instruction should be brief and built into a schedule, with established routines for engaging with the content. Set clear and consistent expectations for students when they interact with videos.

Asynchronous instruction is just one piece of a complete learning experience. Plan opportunities for students to interact and share their learning. Students might post in discussion boards, meet virtually in small groups to complete shared activities, or debrief learning in whole-group synchronous sessions.

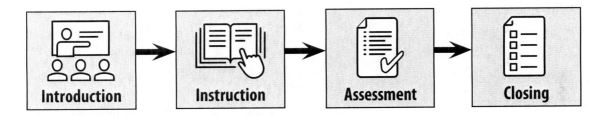

| Introduction | Instruction | Assessment | Closing |

Introduction

A consistent introduction provides continuity and builds consistency. At the beginning of the recording, be certain students know what materials they will need for the lesson and activity.

Instruction

Begin instruction with clear objectives, and define a purpose for the lesson. Keep the recorded lesson interactive by asking questions and encouraging students to pause the video to compose responses or complete brief activities.

Closing

As with synchronous learning, a consistent lesson closing and summary of next steps helps students be successful with independent learning. Be sure to provide step-by-step assignments in writing (including pictures when appropriate) and orally.

Tips for Distance-Learning Environments (cont.)

Asynchronous Instruction (cont.)

Assessment

Assessment of student understanding happens after asynchronous instruction. Assign post-instruction activities that provide opportunities for students to apply their learning from the recorded lessons and demonstrate their understanding of lesson objectives. Follow up with students individually to provide feedback and reteach as necessary.

Which Instruction to Use

This chart provides options for the best uses of synchronous and asynchronous instructional time:

Synchronous Instruction	Asynchronous Instruction
Whole Group • Introduce new concepts. • Teach strategies. • Launch projects or instructional units. • Hold class discussions. • Conduct short read-alouds for shared discussion.	**Whole Group** • Create videos of direct instruction mini-lessons to share with students. • Share videos from online sources that model skills and processes. • Use a website, such as Flipgrid, to share daily read-alouds with students.
Small Group • Hold small groups for collaborative work. • Provide time for small-group discussions.	**Small Group** • Have students collaborate through online documents or platforms.
Other Purposes • Check for understanding. • Set learning goals. • Hold office hours.	**Other Purposes** • Have students respond to one another's work. • Provide independent options for learning through choice boards.

Independent Learning

Provide opportunities for students to engage in independent activities, such as project-based learning. (See page 12 for more information.) After direct instruction has been provided and student understanding has been assessed, engage students in projects to transfer their learning to new situations and environments. Offer students options for completing work and demonstrating their learning. Students may want to complete tasks in writing, record podcasts or videos, or create models or posters to share their learning.

When possible, use an application to convert PDFs into fillable forms. That way, students can complete activities independently and submit their work via sharing platforms. This allows for more meaningful teacher and peer review and feedback.

During this time, you can also keep students engaged in learning and provide meaningful feedback during scheduled one-on-one conferences. While meeting with students, give them opportunities to share what they are interested in learning more about. Providing personalized attention to students will keep them motivated.

Finally, invite students to change their learning environments by completing activities outside or in new locations. Students can successfully engage in reading activities, science experiments, and games in varied locations.

Hybrid Learning

Hybrid learning is a myriad of combinations that can include in-person instruction, virtual instruction (both synchronous and asynchronous), and independent learning. Develop consistent learning plans that transition among all methods of learning based on your school and/or district plans. For example, have students complete activities independently, with partners, or in centers while you provide mini-lessons or complete assessments with small groups of students. Engage families in the learning process by assigning activities, tasks, and projects as school-home extensions. Keep the learning targets for each learning environment clear, and use similar methods across the varying environments to connect the learning for students.

Key Practices for Virtual Classrooms
Project-Based Learning

One method to fully engage students in hybrid learning is through project-based learning (PBL). This instructional strategy allows students to explore the content, explain what they've learned, and apply their new learning to other areas. This chart highlights the benefits of PBL and why it fits well into distance-learning environments.

	Explore	**Explain**	**Apply**
Summary	Students research and explore information through reading, observing, analyzing pictures, watching videos, and so on.	Students share what they've learned through presentations, written summaries, mini-lessons for other students, guided experiments, etc.	Students take what they learned and apply it to further activities and projects.
What Teachers Do	• set expectations • share guiding questions • provide space and opportunities for learning	• set up frameworks for sharing sessions • provide opportunities for presentations • encourage conversation • allow for collaboration	• set clear expectations for activities • provide evaluation tools at onset • create cycle for feedback
What Students Do	• discover • question • gather • identify • navigate • respond	• teach others • fill in the gaps • tie information together • help organize information for others	• create projects • make creations • respond creatively • experiment • collect data and share

Culturally Responsive Learning

Culturally and linguistically responsive (CLR) teaching expert Dr. Sharroky Hollie (2020) defines a culturally responsive mindset in the following way: "Being culturally responsive is an approach to living life in a way that practices the validation and affirmation of different cultures for the purposes of moving beyond race and moving below the superficial focus on culture." When educators use culturally responsive teaching strategies, students are more engaged, which in turn helps them to be more successful academically.

As Hollie (2020) states, culturally responsive teaching helps students understand "when to use the most appropriate cultural and linguistic behaviors for any situation without losing who they are culturally and linguistically." This happens when educators Validate, Affirm, Build, and Bridge within their learning environments. Whether learning is in-person, virtual, or a combination of the two, specifically plan to "VABB" in learning activities. When you **validate** students' home environments, you legitimize their home cultures and languages. **Affirmation** works to end the negative stereotypes associated with non-mainstream cultures. Once this initial work has been started, **build** deeper relationships with students by showing them that you care and understand their home cultures. Finally, give students the skills they need for success by showing them the **bridges** to mainstream culture.

What Is VABB?

Validate

Affirm

Build

Bridge

In learning environments where educators take into account their students' home cultures and languages, students feel empowered. They begin to see that they can do and be whatever they want. To further this feeling, incorporate diverse literature from varied cultures so students can identify with the characters and see themselves in the texts, and ask students open-ended questions that guide them to find connections between their lives and what they are learning.

Key Practices for Virtual Classrooms <small>(cont.)</small>
Social-Emotional Learning

Educators who purposely focus on social-emotional learning (SEL) and the affective aspects of what students are learning enhance "students' capacity to integrate skills, attitudes, and behaviors to deal effectively and ethically with daily tasks and challenges" (CASEL 2020). Today's world is increasingly complex. Students need to learn how to problem-solve and make the difficult decisions that face them. Not only does a focus on SEL help students face difficult life situations, but identifying and discussing "emotions, thoughts, and behaviors" (CASEL 2020) can help students be more confident and optimistic.

Teachers can connect SEL strategies to classroom activities. The Collaborative for Academic, Social, and Emotional Learning (CASEL) describes these commonly recognized competencies: self-awareness, self-management, social awareness, relationship skills, and responsible decision-making. Educators can create anchor charts that align to the competencies and refer to those charts when activities align to them.

CASEL's Competencies

Self-Awareness

Self-Management

Social Awareness

Relationship Skills

Responsible Decision-Making

While teaching, have students recognize and name emotions in their own actions and within the texts they read. When teaching in virtual environments, regular check-ins with students allow for them to grow in their understanding of themselves and how to navigate the ever-changing world around them. Whether teaching remotely or in-person, consistently and authentically celebrate students' accomplishments.

How to Use This Resource

Choose a strategy and give it a try! Some strategies include student activity pages, which are provided in Appendix B as well as digitally. (See page 96 for more information about the Digital Resources.)

This introductory text provides a brief description of the strategy.

Ideas for application of the strategy are provided for three grade ranges. Be sure to check out all the options!

Additional resources are provided to support your teaching of the strategy.

These notes are key things to think about when using the strategy.

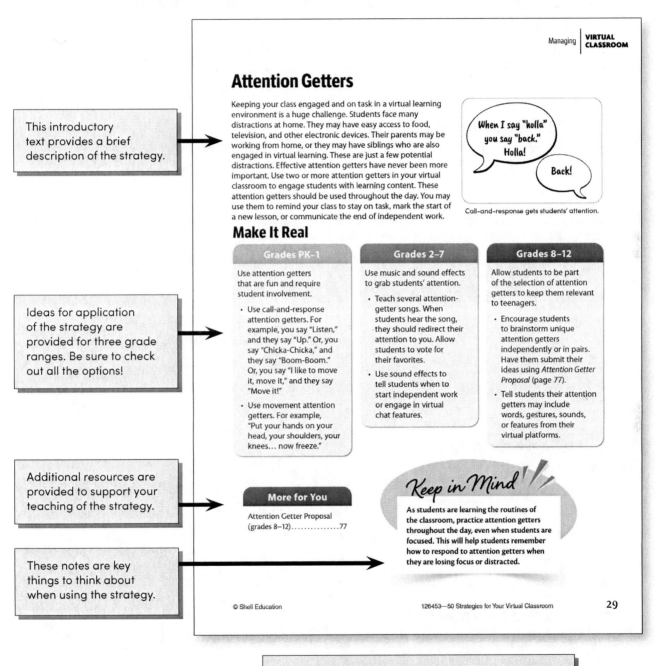

Managing | **VIRTUAL CLASSROOM**

Attention Getters

Keeping your class engaged and on task in a virtual learning environment is a huge challenge. Students face many distractions at home. They may have easy access to food, television, and other electronic devices. Their parents may be working from home, or they may have siblings who are also engaged in virtual learning. These are just a few potential distractions. Effective attention getters have never been more important. Use two or more attention getters in your virtual classroom to engage students with learning content. These attention getters should be used throughout the day. You may use them to remind your class to stay on task, mark the start of a new lesson, or communicate the end of independent work.

When I say "holla" you say "back." Holla!

Back!

Call-and-response gets students' attention.

Make It Real

Grades PK–1	Grades 2–7	Grades 8–12
Use attention getters that are fun and require student involvement.	Use music and sound effects to grab students' attention.	Allow students to be part of the selection of attention getters to keep them relevant to teenagers.
• Use call-and-response attention getters. For example, you say "Listen," and they say "Up." Or, you say "Chicka-Chicka," and they say "Boom-Boom." Or, you say "I like to move it, move it," and they say "Move it!" • Use movement attention getters. For example, "Put your hands on your head, your shoulders, your knees... now freeze."	• Teach several attention-getter songs. When students hear the song, they should redirect their attention to you. Allow students to vote for their favorites. • Use sound effects to tell students when to start independent work or engage in virtual chat features.	• Encourage students to brainstorm unique attention getters independently or in pairs. Have them submit their ideas using *Attention Getter Proposal* (page 77). • Tell students their attention getters may include words, gestures, sounds, or features from virtual platforms.

More for You

Attention Getter Proposal
(grades 8–12) 77

Keep in Mind

As students are learning the routines of the classroom, practice attention getters throughout the day, even when students are focused. This will help students remember how to respond to attention getters when they are losing focus or distracted.

Refer to the Technology Notes in Appendix C for suggested apps or websites to support each strategy.

Strategies Table of Contents

At-Home Classroom

All teachers have specific preferences when it comes to their classrooms. Wall decorations, desk positioning, and lighting all play a part in your learning environment. Believe it or not, the same thing goes for virtual teaching! Think about your space and the options you have, and create your own optimal teacher space. Provide yourself with a clean background and a place to write where students can see (a whiteboard or chart paper behind you or a document camera). Ensure that you have enough light in the room so students can see your face. Check to be certain that students can read things you show in your camera. These details will give you confidence as you create the perfect distance-teaching space.

This space has good light and a whiteboard.

Make It Real

Grades PK–3

Younger students have shorter attention spans, so be sure to eliminate all distractions.

- Keep students engaged by focusing your camera on your face.

- Ensure that you have good lighting and a plain background (no shiny posters, animals, or family members).

Grades 4–8

To better interact with students, maintain easy access to various materials.

- Use a whiteboard, chart paper, or document camera to write or draw so lessons are more than just lectures.

- Store all your necessary materials within reach so you don't have to leave the screen when switching gears.

Grades 9–12

These tech-savvy students will get frustrated with technological obstacles.

- Practice navigating the technology you plan to use prior to a lesson. Ask trustworthy students for help if you need it.

- Recognize that your virtual teaching won't be perfect and move quickly past any stumbles to mitigate student frustrations.

More for You

Level Up and Lighten Up video

tcmpub.digital/50/athome

Keep in Mind

When using a whiteboard or chart paper, write in dark colors and with large lettering. Take pictures of what you write, and post the pictures for students to reference later. You can also use a document camera (or even a cell phone) to share with students, or share your computer screen with the group.

Introduction Videos

You want to get to know your students, but they also want to get to know you! Record videos that introduce you, the virtual classroom, and some basic expectations. Discuss your passions, work experience, home life, teaching philosophies, and other interesting facts. Then, make one or two videos that explain your virtual teaching model and classroom. Finally, introduce some of the ground rules and basic principles that govern your learning environment. These videos will help students (and families) navigate your class. (You can make videos throughout the year so students can continue to get to know you.)

Be sure to share things you love with students!

Make It Real

Grades PK–1	Grades 2–5	Grades 6–12
Primary students will likely feel nervous, so ease their stress by presenting yourself as open and engaging.	Help students get familiar with you as well as with distance learning.	Encourage positive attitudes toward distance learning by displaying confidence.

Grades PK–1

- Get creative with your videos by moving your camera around your house or using props.
- Excite students with fun or silly facts about both yourself and your class.

Grades 2–5

- Include interesting facts about yourself in your introduction videos.
- Present students with a clear path to navigating your virtual classroom.

Grades 6–12

- Introduce yourself in a natural, comfortable way so students can meet the real you.
- Introduce your virtual classroom and talk about your expectations, but acknowledge that students may need time to find success.

More for You

Introduce Yourself video

tcmpub.digital/50/introduction

Keep in Mind

Stay focused on the camera when speaking so students feel like you're making eye contact. Use a handheld device or your computer to record your videos and then upload them to your virtual classroom. You can also use an online platform to record and post videos.

Home Norms

Just like you need to set up your at-home classroom, so do your students. Work with students to create simple and productive norms for completing their work at home. Provide norms such as finding a quiet spot, clearing a space for papers, and keeping all supplies together in one space. These norms will help students build their own learning spaces. Keep in mind that students have a wide variety of environments for setting up their at-home learning spaces. Help each student discover ways to create the best spot for themselves. And ensure that students are not put into situations where they are comparing home-learning environments with one another. These questions will help you support families when creating home norms:

- Where will supplies be stored?

- How can devices stay charged?

- How can students get help (from the teacher and at home)?

This student is ready to start sixth grade!

Make It Real

Grades PK–2	Grades 3–5	Grades 6–12
For younger students, utilize family support and a positive classroom environment.	Provide these students with structure to help them stay organized and focused.	Encourage older students to be flexible but also to establish self-discipline.
• Verify that students have parents or caretakers who can help them establish their learning spaces. • Send families emails that include recommended daily supplies and other communications.	• Encourage students to stay organized, and provide students with supply lists and schedules in advance. • Give students a way to ask you for advice on constructing their at-home classrooms.	• Remind students to maintain easy access to all their supplies in case lessons change unexpectedly. • Advise students to bring their supplies to their learning spaces and nothing else (no cell phones, pets, tablets, etc.).

Keep in Mind

Share supply lists and at-home classroom suggestions as email attachments and also post them as virtual announcements. Make sure all families can access this key information. Revist the norms frequently to help students stay focused and organized.

Fun and Physical Activity

In traditional classrooms, there are both spontaneous and planned moments of fun and celebration, and students have scheduled opportunities to participate in physical activity through recess, physical education, or collaborative work. Make sure you include these types of activities in your distance-learning classroom as well. Schedule physical activity breaks for students each day. Suggest a variety of ways for students to engage in movement activities no matter their space limitations. Consider including these moments in your synchronous instruction whenever possible. Also, include physical activities in asynchronous assignments as much as possible to increase time students spend away from their monitors.

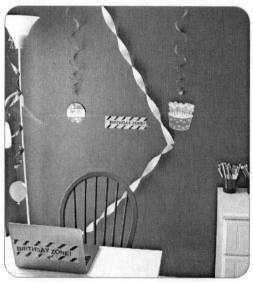

Decorating adds fun to virtual classrooms.

Make It Real

Grades PK–3

Younger students will stay engaged if they can have fun.

- Take a break, and have students start a dance party, run around their houses, make silly faces into their cameras, etc.
- Celebrate holidays and birthdays by having students adorn their backgrounds or create themed projects with materials from home.

Grades 4–8

Foster the social-emotional well-being of these students with group activities.

- Encourage students to dress up or decorate in celebration of holidays.
- Post surveys that ask students for their opinions about what activities to do or how to celebrate. Or, use *Celebration Time!* (page 69) to ask students how they'd like to celebrate.

Grades 9–12

Older students will appreciate breaks from their heavy workloads.

- Implement icebreakers and brain breaks (see page 34) in the virtual classroom.
- Share an occasional picture or video that's bound to make your students laugh.

More for You

Celebration Time!
(grades 4–12) 69

Keep in Mind

Be sure to include some celebrations and physical activities in your virtual learning schedule. Some students may feel self-conscious about moving around on camera. Allow for all students to participate in ways that help them feel comfortable.

Weekly & Daily Schedules

Following guidance provided by your school or district, create a weekly schedule that includes synchronous, asynchronous, and independent learning activities. The more consistent your schedule, the easier it will be for students and families to follow. To provide students with even more structure, create and share a daily schedule. Ensure that both schedules remain as consistent as possible. Teach and regularly review your schedules. Remember that shorter periods of synchronous instruction will support students in remaining engaged.

Sample Daily Schedule

9:00	live	reading whole class
9:45	live	writing in small groups
10:00	recorded	watch music or art video
10:15		Break Time!
10:30	live	math whole class
11:00	independent	math classwork and fun challenge
11:45		LUNCH!
1:00	live	science or social studies whole class
1:30	recorded	watch science or social studies video
1:45	independent	silent reading
2:15		Break Time!
2:30	live	reading in small groups
3:15		dismissal

Schedules should be clear and consistent.

Make It Real

Grades PK–2

Younger students will need designated time for synchronous and small-group instruction.

- Utilize short periods of synchronous instruction in engaging, meaningful ways.
- Work with students one-on-one or in small groups to identify and address learning gaps.
- Ask families to support their students, if possible, during asynchronous learning.

Grades 3–8

Find balance among teaching models to best engage students.

- Structure independent learning with easy-to-understand directions and meaningful activities.
- Encourage students to interact with their peers in new ways within the virtual classroom.

Grades 9–12

Allow students to take control of their learning, but remember to provide them with support and encouragement.

- Build independent learning around deep, challenging activities.
- Engage reluctant learners during synchronous learning and guide them toward success when they're working on their own.
- Include time in your weekly schedule for students to get one-on-one or small-group support from you.

More for You

Weekly Schedule video
tcmpub.digital/50/schedule

Keep in Mind

Share and update your schedule through announcements on your virtual classroom page or through daily/weekly emails. Be sure to highlight schedule changes with bold or brightly colored fonts as well as a separate post acknowledging the change.

Creating Playlists

What can unite students in all classrooms? Music! Most students have bands, artists, and songs they like, so music is a great tool for the virtual classroom. Work with students to build music playlists for use during the virtual learning day. This will incentivize and excite students by introducing a new dimension to at-home learning. Create playlists for different times within their virtual days (transitions, independent work time, etc.). Give students opportunities to share their student-created playlists. Sharing engages students and helps them discover like-minded peers, which will in turn create a more welcoming classroom environment.

YouTube allows students to create free playlists.

Make It Real

Grades PK–1

Create playlists with students so they feel like part of the process.

1. Have students submit songs to you.

2. Compile those songs into playlists for the whole class.

3. Play the music on your own device at the appropriate times.

Grades 2–5

While some of these students may be familiar with creating playlists, others will need help.

- Share resources, such as short how-tos or videos, to help students navigate various music platforms and playlists.

- Discuss concepts such as the difference between a good transition song and a good homework song. Have students complete *My Playlist* (page 70) as they think about their options.

Grades 6–12

These students will most likely have their own devices and be familiar with how to create music playlists.

- Encourage students to choose songs that match the allotted time during the school day. Have students complete *Playlist Ideas* (page 71) to describe their choices.

- Ask students to experiment and evaluate which songs work best at which times, and why.

More for You

Keep in Mind

For students who do not already have access to a music library, several free music sites allow people to create music playlists at no cost.

Identity Maps

Helping students meet and get to know their peers is a major part of in-person learning, and the same goes for your online classroom. One way to develop your classroom community is to have students create digital identity maps. In the center of their maps, students can share pictures of themselves with their names. Around the pictures, students describe themselves using words and pictures. They should explain who they are, what they like to do, what their favorite things are, their fears and annoyances, and any interesting facts about themselves. Students can easily share these identity maps in multiple ways. If you are teaching synchronously, students can send you their digital identity maps and explain their maps while they are on your screen. For asynchronous learning, students can post their maps to an online board and interact with one another.

Evelyn used Jamboard to share about herself!

Make It Real

Grades PK–2

Work with younger students to explore the various technology platforms they can use to make their maps.

- Help students make their maps colorful and engaging.
- Encourage students to ask for help from their families to best utilize the technology.

Grades 3–7

Allow students to be flexible and creative as they make and present their maps.

- Remind students to think outside the box with their pictures and words. Encourage them to find ways to make their maps unique.
- Inspire creative thinking with examples from an identity map of your own.

Grades 8–12

Add new dimensions to the activity to engage older students in a meaningful way.

- Ask students why they chose the descriptors they did and what external factors influenced their decisions.
- Challenge students to create identity maps for fictional characters, historical people, or peers using the template on page 72.

More for You

Keep in Mind

Students can use free online platforms to insert pictures and words when creating their maps. Students who prefer hands-on activities can create their maps using art supplies and paper.

Caption This!

Humor can unify students and create a more engaging learning environment, especially when building rapport and community in a virtual learning environment. For this activity, share a funny picture. Encourage students to use their creative senses of humor to write captions and share them with their peers. If you're teaching synchronously, have students share through the chat feature. If you're working asynchronously, have them post captions through an online platform. To further build peer relationships, students can "like" captions to convey their approval for particular captions. Utilize these features, if possible, to help students engage with their peers in a fun, positive way.

How we feel about Mondays

Make It Real

Grades PK–2	Grades 3–7	Grades 8–12
Inspire creative captions by helping students understand the picture and the purpose of the caption.	Outline clear rules, but also allow students to have fun.	Challenge students to create captions that are widely liked and intellectual.
• Discuss the picture's comedic value. Ask a few students why they think the picture is funny.	• Remind students to be respectful and positive. Praise captions that are both funny and use appropriate language.	• Raise the stakes by rewarding the best captions with bragging rights or a silly prize.
• Have students brainstorm key words that come to mind when they see the picture. Provide a list of these words for students as they create captions for the picture.	• Ask students to draw their own funny pictures on *My Captions* (page 73). Then, have students share their pictures and write captions for one another's pictures.	• Encourage students to use literary devices (simile, double entendre, paradox, etc.) in their captions.

More for You

My Captions (grades 3–7)...73

Keep in Mind

If you're unsure about how to find good images, try these search terms on browser search engines to get you started:

- "funny animal pictures"
- "food art for kids"
- "funny superhero cartoons for kids"
- "caption contest pictures"

Show-and-Tell

Another fun way to help students get to know one another is through show-and-tell. Provide students with opportunities to share various things that are important to them during synchronous learning time. By giving students time to share their special items, favorite reading spots, things they love, pets, favorite toys, or new video games, you are getting to know them and helping them get to know one another. If sharing during a live lesson is not possible, have students record short videos and post them on an online platform instead.

Students share favorite toys
in a Zoom meeting.

Make It Real

Grades PK–2	Grades 3–5	Grades 6–12
Set guidelines so younger students know how long to share.	Help students find unique items to present in a clear, engaging way.	Encourage older students to be creative with what they present.
• Keep presentations short, ideally around a minute long. • Provide a sentence frame for students to use during their sharing time.	• Give students lots of ideas on what items, pets, or locations they can share. Encourage students to ask others for help when deciding what to share. • Remind students to practice their presentations ahead of time.	• Ask students to show what books, movies, sports, and music they are interested in. • Have students explain the significance of each item or tell the story of where it came from.

Keep in Mind

If teaching synchronously, unmute and allow each student to share. If working asynchronously, use an online platform so students can post short videos or pictures of their items.

Classroom Surveys

Every student wants to find peers who share their interests and opinions. Creating survey questions for students to complete quickly is one way to get to know students while helping them bond over similarities. To provide students with opportunities to build connections and relationships with their classmates, ask fun, interesting, and age-appropriate questions. For example: *What animal do you really like? What do you enjoy studying? Which class are you most excited about this year?* After gathering the responses, share the classroom survey questions and their results with students.

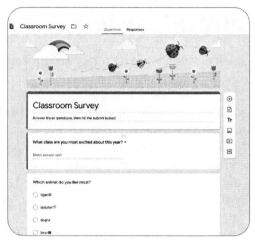

Fun, cute, short surveys build community.

Make It Real

Grades PK–2	Grades 3–8	Grades 9–12
For young students, ask fun, lighthearted questions that help students find commonalities with their peers.	Balance fun and simple questions with deeper, more interesting ones.	Engage older students by featuring deeper, more relevant topics in the survey.

Grades PK–2

- Ask questions, such as *What is your favorite animal?* and *Which ice cream flavor is best?*
- Connect the survey to school by asking students to list their favorite subjects or styles of learning.

Grades 3–8

- Include questions, such as *What is your favorite food?* but also, *If you could go anywhere in the world, where would you go?*
- Encourage students to create their own surveys using *My Survey* (page 74). Then have them conduct their surveys and graph the results.

Grades 9–12

- Discover your students' plans for the future, favorite music and movies, and interesting personal facts.
- Add some controversial questions, such as whether pineapple belongs on pizza or whether social media is too influential. These can be great persuasive writing prompts also.

More for You

My Survey (grades 3–8) 74

Keep in Mind

Use various types of survey questions (multiple choice, fill-in-the-blank, etc.) to keep students engaged and interested. When sharing results, you can present them synchronously by sharing your screen or asynchronously by posting screenshots.

Social Contracts

Establish an agreement for your virtual learning environment. Provide time for students to offer suggestions, make changes, and provide input. Revisit social contracts as students become more familiar with how virtual classrooms work. As you work with students, keep in mind that classroom contracts should consider all students and their varying learning environments. Considering the comfort of students and their families is imperative for creating successful virtual learning environments.

Pictures make contracts easier to read.

Make It Real

Grades PK–1	Grades 2–5	Grades 6–12
Keep social contracts short and sweet for young learners. Use pictures to support the contracts.	Encourage collaboration in the creation of the contract.	Encourage students to take ownership of social contracts.

Grades PK–1

- Your social contract may be a simple statement, such as *As I learn, I will show respect to myself and others.*

- Your social contract may be a list of dos and don'ts, such as: *Do raise your hand. Do share your thoughts. Do listen to others. Don't talk over classmates.*

Grades 2–5

1. Have students work in small groups to organize their thoughts using *Social Contract Brainstorm* (page 75).

2. Review the small-group ideas as a class and choose some rules to use. Post these ideas in a spot students can access virtually or see in your at-home classroom.

Grades 6–12

- Ask students what classroom rules they have found useful in the past. Have them explain why they have found these rules useful.

- Have students brainstorm rules that they may need specifically for virtual settings and create a class contract together.

More for You

Keep in Mind

Review social contracts at the start of synchronous learning sessions to set students up for success. Create a dynamic version of your social contract online, and allow students to sign it digitally using their names or emojis. When brainstorming, think about using online polling functions to vote on classroom rules or other parts of the contract.

Virtual Greetings

Establish fun and friendly virtual greetings. Use greetings to welcome students into their virtual classrooms. Think of these greetings as virtual high fives, handshakes, or hugs. Give students opportunities to share their ideas for virtual greetings. Encourage them to use their savvy with online interactions to create unique virtual greetings. Involve students by having them participate as virtual greeters. You may want to create a virtual greeter "job." Assign the job to a different student each week. Work to make virtual greetings a quick part of the opening routine of the classroom.

Don't underestimate the value of a smile and wave.

Make It Real

Grades PK–1	Grades 2–5	Grades 6–12
Use gestures to help younger students remember virtual greetings.	Provide clear rules for student greeters.	Create greeting committees to get student buy-in.
• Each time a student joins, wave your hand and say, "Welcome, friend!" Have each student respond to your greeting with a thumbs-up.	• Tell student greeters to unmute themselves and greet students as they sign in. Remind greeters to use appropriate virtual greetings.	• Assign several students to the committees. Encourage greeting committees to create unique ways of saying hello. Ask students to "name" their virtual greetings.
• Hold your finger to your mouth to make the "shh" sign and say, "Don't forget to mute your audio."	• Gather student ideas for virtual greetings through the *Virtual Greeting Proposal* (page 76).	• Let students know whether they should be greeting students orally or through chat features.

More for You

Virtual Greeting Proposal (grades 2–5)...............76

Virtual Greetings video

tcmpub.digital/50/greetings

Keep in Mind

Review all student-created virtual greetings before they are presented to the class to avoid disruption or inappropriate greetings. Students may have different levels of comfort when interacting with you and their peers. Be thoughtful about this as you use virtual greetings.

Attention Getters

Keeping your class engaged and on task in a virtual learning environment is a huge challenge. Students face many distractions at home. They may have easy access to food, television, and other electronic devices. Their parents may be working from home, or they may have siblings who are also engaged in virtual learning. These are just a few potential distractions. Effective attention getters have never been more important. Use two or more attention getters in your virtual classroom to engage students with learning content. These attention getters should be used throughout the day. You may use them to remind your class to stay on task, mark the start of a new lesson, or communicate the end of independent work.

Use call-and-response to get students' attention.

Make It Real

Grades PK–1	Grades 2–7	Grades 8–12
Use attention getters that are fun and require student involvement.	Use music and sound effects to grab students' attention.	Allow students to be part of the selection of attention getters to keep them relevant to teenagers.

Grades PK–1

Use attention getters that are fun and require student involvement.

- Use call-and-response attention getters. For example, you say "Listen," and they say "Up." Or, you say "Chicka-Chicka," and they say "Boom-Boom." Or, you say "I like to move it, move it," and they say "Move it!"
- Use movement attention getters. For example, "Put your hands on your head, your shoulders, your knees…now freeze."

Grades 2–7

Use music and sound effects to grab students' attention.

- Teach several attention-getter songs. When students hear the song, they should redirect their attention to you. Allow students to vote for their favorites.
- Use sound effects to tell students when to start independent work or engage in virtual chat features.

Grades 8–12

Allow students to be part of the selection of attention getters to keep them relevant to teenagers.

- Encourage students to brainstorm unique attention getters independently or in pairs. Have them submit their ideas using *Attention Getter Proposal* (page 77).
- Tell students their attention getters may include words, gestures, sounds, or features from their virtual platforms.

More for You

Keep in Mind

As students are learning the routines of the classroom, practice attention getters throughout the day, even when students are focused. This will help students remember how to respond to attention getters when they are losing focus or distracted.

Bell Ringers

Start your day right! Begin class with authentic learning problems or fun thinking-skills activities. Bell ringer assignments provide students with activities that engage them at the very start of synchronous learning sessions. Bell ringer activities often focus on content that has been covered. Or, they may be focused on critical or creative thinking. Activities are designed to start during the greeting at the beginning of class and last for less than 10 minutes. Ensure bell ringers are content specific, support previous learning, and are attainable tasks. Some examples to consider include the following:

- math word problems
- vocabulary activities, such as word ladders
- short writing prompts
- brainstorming and creative thinking

> As you log on, jot down a quick list of *many*, varied, and *unusual* things that are ROUND.
>
> This activity gets students thinking as soon as class begins.

Make It Real

Grades PK–1

Bell ringers may focus on phonics to get some extra practice in.

- Ask students to write rhyming words or phrases. This helps students practice phonics and creative thinking.
- Ask students to complete picture or word sorts. These activities will also help build critical-thinking skills.

Grades 2–7

Bell ringers may include quick writes or prewriting activities.

1. Present a paragraph for students to read. Ask students to jot down their opinions about the text.
2. Have students add reasons for their opinions.
3. Have two students quickly share their opinions and reasons at the end of the bell-ringer session.

Grades 8–12

Bell ringers may focus on motivating students and helping them focus.

- Have students list facts, figures, data, information, vocabulary words, or other concepts related to what you've been studying in class. Encourage them to record these on a sharing platform so they can add on to others' ideas.
- Spark creative thinking by letting students free draw, brainstorm, or free write as they get settled.

More for You

Bell Ringer video

tcmpub.digital/50/bellringers

Keep in Mind

To keep students on task, think about using music, sound effects, or a timer to let students know when they have two minutes left to complete their bell ringer problems or responses. Don't let these opening activities eat into your instructional time.

Virtual Games

When it comes to keeping students engaged, creativity is key! Adapt games students are familiar with to virtual learning environments. For example, try playing virtual games of Simon Says to capture students' attention. Ask your students to respond to Simon Says prompts just as they would during an in-person game. When you say "Simon says smile," students should smile. If you say "Wave your hands," students should keep their hands still. Games can help refocus students on new learning content or practice classroom rules.

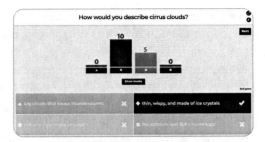

Kahoot! helps you easily create engaging virtual games.

Make It Real

Grades PK–1	Grades 2–5	Grades 6–12
Clearly define the game's rules each time you play.	Encourage students help decide which games to play.	These students are less likely than younger students to want to play physical games in virtual environments.
• Model for students what they should do if you say or don't say "Simon says." • Allow students to lead games you've played with them already.	• Have students lead games, such as virtual Simon Says, as well as other games they suggest to you. • Work with students to think of other physical games you can bring into your virtual classroom. Or, give them time to make up new games related to what they're learning.	• Work with students to think of fun games to break up the learning. Let them decide which sound interesting and engaging. • You may choose to allow students to abstain from participating. They can sit quietly or read while the other students play.

Keep in Mind

If asking students to use chat features in games, make sure all students understand how to access and utilize chat features. See pages 93–95 for information on apps and websites you can use to create games.

Scavenger Hunts

Every student loves a good scavenger hunt! Have students hunt for things in their learning spaces that are connected to the topic, content, or vocabulary used within a lesson. For example, if discussing types of measurement, ask students to find objects that are less than four inches (10 centimeters) in diameter. During synchronous learning, students can then hold their items up to the camera and explain in the chat how the items connect to the lesson. During asynchronous learning, students can post pictures of their objects and include descriptive captions.

Scavenger Hunt!!

FIND A CUBE

This scavenger hunt makes geometry real.

Make It Real

Grades PK–2	Grades 3–5	Grades 6–12
Make the scavenger hunt exciting and interactive.	Connect this fun activity to the subject matter in an interesting way.	Help older students enjoy this activity by adding a challenge or twist.
• Challenge students to find objects in a designated amount of time, such as less than a minute. • Have students talk in small groups to explain how their objects connect to the lesson.	• Encourage students to think outside the box when searching for items to share. • Give students suggestions to get them started, while at the same time encouraging them to find objects and connections that their peers have not.	• Ask students to find objects that fit difficult size or color guidelines. • Reward students who find objects that have the most meaningful connections to the lesson.

More for You

Scavenger Hunt video

tcmpub.digital/50/scavengerhunt

Keep in Mind

If sharing asynchronously, have students post their captioned pictures in the classroom feed or use an online platform to share and interact with student ideas.

Movement Is Magic

Allowing students to interact with you and their classmates in creative ways is an essential component to virtual teaching. Whenever possible, have students interact using movement. For example, create physical actions to represent new vocabulary words, or have students stand or sit to share responses. Students can raise their hands or give thumbs-up/thumbs-down in response to questions. Students can respond through movement using their cameras during synchronous learning or through videos in asynchronous and independent learning. Moving around will keep students excited and help them actively participate.

Even a simple thumbs-up keeps students engaged.

Make It Real

Grades PK–4	Grades 5–8	Grades 9–12
Identify clear rules, but allow students to have fun with their physical responses.	Make movement a normal part of your virtual learning model so students become more comfortable with it.	While older students may be cynical at first, movement will keep them engaged.
• Explain what each physical response means before asking students to participate. • Encourage students to be fully involved and enjoy the physical activity.	• Ask questions that your students can easily answer using physical responses. • Have students practice physical responses in a variety of subjects and settings.	• Remind students that physical activity is a good way to break up long periods of screen time. • Listen to students' ideas on possible physical responses. (They may have good suggestions you haven't thought of yet.)

Keep in Mind

Be sure to turn off screen share when using this strategy so that students can view the movement and physical responses of their peers. Consider allowing students to abstain from participating for personal reasons, such as being introverted, but encourage them to stay engaged in other ways.

Brain Breaks

Screen fatigue is real. Staring into a computer monitor gets boring, and students need time to de-stress, raise their heart rates, and so on. In the brick-and-mortar classroom, students get occasional breaks, and the virtual classroom should be no different! To make breaks both fun and meaningful, assign interactive, short (five minutes or less) activities for students to do independently or in breakout rooms. For example, have students brainstorm words that include double consonants or ways to write without using a pencil or pen. Brain breaks can require physical movement, such as running in place or writing, but brain teasers, mental challenges, mindfulness moments, and creativity breaks are beneficial as well.

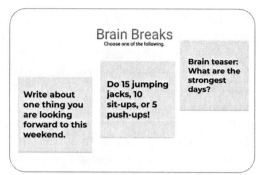

Brain breaks can be physical or can practice thinking skills.

Make It Real

Grades PK–1

Younger students have lots of energy, so play music and let them get up and move around!

- Find brain breaks that let students leave their learning spaces or exercise in place.

- Select students to explain what they liked best about each brain break as everyone settles back in their seats, ready to learn.

Grades 2–4

Promote social-emotional growth by letting students collaborate.

- Put students into breakout sessions, per your school and district policies, so they can work in small groups. Encourage them to work together in productive and fun ways.

- Have each group elect a spokesperson to share their process and their funniest brain-break moments.

Grades 5–12

Motivate older students with challenging tasks and fun rewards.

- Choose tricky brain teasers or seemingly impossible physical tasks for your students to try. Then, praise students who succeed and offer them bragging rights or some kind of reward.

- Have students use *Give Me a Break* (page 78) to suggest their own brain breaks. Share these student-created brain breaks with the class for some fun and celebration.

Keep in Mind

Not sure where to start? Use these online searches to find some brain-break ideas:

- "brain breaks for kids"
- "brain break activities PDF"
- "virtual brain breaks"
- "challenging brain breaks"

More for You

"I Wonder" Boards

When students ask, respond to, or ponder questions about what they're learning, they are more likely to stay engaged. Use an "I Wonder" board to provide students with a place to collaborate and share their wonderings about a new topic. Create your class board in an online platform by writing a topic or idea at the top or in the center of the board. Then, students can add their wonderings to the virtual wall, like sticky notes on chart paper.

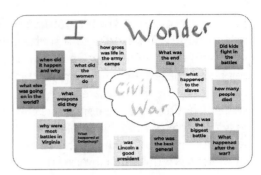

These students used Jamboard to ask questions.

Make It Real

Grades PK–3	Grades 4–8	Grades 9–12
Help your students navigate online platforms.	Give clear expectations and instructions to make the activity effective.	Challenge students to pose deep, complex wonderings.
• Demonstrate how to post wonderings during synchronous instruction. • Encourage students to practice posting and viewing the board during asynchronous or independent time.	• Model how you want students to write their posts (i.e., phrases or full sentences). • Tell students how many wonderings they can and should post. Or, encourage them to post as many as they want. Students will benefit from having clear expectations.	• Encourage students to think of various meaningful questions rather than simply posting the first one that comes to mind. • Ask students to find and post the answers to their peers' wonderings either during the lesson or after it.

Keep in Mind

Monitor student posts as they appear on the "I Wonder" board so you can pose additional questions, identify common themes, understand students' reasoning, and check for understanding.

Think-Pair-Share

In the world of virtual learning, students need purposeful and authentic opportunities for socialization. One of the best ways to foster this student-to-student interaction is with think-pair-share activities. Using various partnering strategies, have students communicate with partners to reflect and share about topics or content. Pairs can work together using assigned chat buddies, in breakout rooms, or in partner-assigned online documents. Then, have students share their thoughts with the whole group. This partner sharing will foster social-emotional well-being as well as keep students invested in learning.

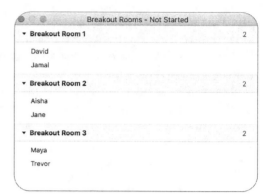

Breakout rooms work well for pairing students.

Make It Real

Grades PK–2	Grades 3–8	Grades 9–12
Clarify your expectations for partner discussions.	Students will be eager to discuss with their friends, but try to develop an inclusive classroom community.	Older students will need more time to make deeper connections.
• Model how students should conduct their think-pair-share conversations. Provide students with an example conversation and time to practice. • Help students determine what to share with the whole group so the discussion is meaningful.	• Create partnerships that will be positive and productive. • Alternate between assigned partners and student-selected partners so students work with many different classmates.	• During synchronous instruction, allow students to have longer partner discussions. • Encourage students to regularly interact with peers during asynchronous learning, whether through collaborative documents or online platforms.

Keep in Mind

Breakout sessions are small-group "rooms" where students can work with partners and then return to the main virtual class. Learn more about your school and district policies as well as the capabilities of your online meeting platform to use breakout sessions for small-group work.

Phonics Quick Draw

Student engagement often goes up when you gamify learning. Practice phonics in a way that will keep your students on the edges of their seats! After phonics instruction, give students clues for a word that follows a phonics rule. For example, after a lesson on the short *a* vowel sound, you may choose the word *bat*. Your clues might include the following: *I am thinking of a short* a *word. It is an animal that lives in a cave. It sleeps upside down. People often think of it at Halloween.* You may also support your verbal clues with visual clues. During synchronous instruction, students can draw sketches of the word and hold them in front of their cameras.

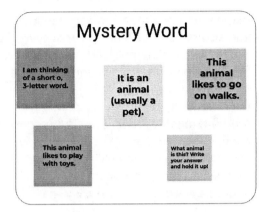

Mystery Word

I am thinking of a short o, 3-letter word.

It is an animal (usually a pet).

This animal likes to go on walks.

This animal likes to play with toys.

What animal is this? Write your answer and hold it up!

Students enjoy finding mystery words.

Make It Real

Grades PK–K	Grade 1	Grade 2
Adjust the activity for the youngest students. Provide additional support when necessary.	Expand the activity to allow students more opportunities to show their knowledge.	Challenge older students to make connections to other vocabulary words.
• Drawing may be difficult for young students. Give them the option of saying the words to family members instead.	• Encourage students to both draw and write the word.	• Ask students to write the word in a sentence. Or have them write lists of words that follow the same phonics rule.
• Give students rhyming words as clues to emphasize the phonics rule you are focusing on.	• After playing the game, have students think more about the word with *Mystery Word* (page 79).	• Have students complete *Guess My Word* (page 80), and then let them alternate as leaders of the game.

More for You

Keep in Mind

There are different ways you can include visuals with this activity. You can print pictures and hold them up to your camera. Or, download pictures to your computer and share your screen with students.

Pick a Poem

Use poetry to improve reading fluency and teach new vocabulary. Provide students with several poems. These can be links online or typed poems shared on your screen. Students may practice reading the poems independently, with partners, or in small groups. Read the poem aloud to model fluent reading for students. Practice the poems chorally during morning meetings or in other synchronous class moments. Then, ask each student to choose a poem. Provide students with opportunities to recite their poetry live or to record themselves reciting their poetry. Discuss the poems and talk about how students felt as they shared them.

Fairy Tale Limericks

A young maiden once lost her shoe
From the beautiful palace she flew
The clock struck midnight
The girl ran in fright
Wearing a dress that was blue.

Three little pigs ran away
And one made a house out of hay
One out of sticks
One out of bricks
Which kept the big bad wolf away.

There was a young girl wearing red
She had a hood on her head
She trekked through the woods
With a basket of goods
To visit her Granny in bed.

By Mary E. Smith, 2015

Rhyming poems engage young readers.

Make It Real

Grades PK–K

For younger students, provide as many opportunities as you can for choral reading. Keep the poems simple and repetitive.

- Before choral reading, model reading the poem several times. Use appropriate rate, volume, and expression.
- Introduce new or difficult words before choral reading. Discuss words again after choral reading.

Grade 1

Give students opportunities to perform their poems.

- Small groups may perform poems for the class together. This performance may be live or recorded.
- Help students to be creative with their performances. Some parts of the poems may be recited chorally, and other parts may have only one reader.

Grade 2

Add new elements to the presentations by older students.

- Encourage students to add hand motions or actions as they present their poems.
- Ask students to select and recite poems that were not presented in class.

Keep in Mind

You may want to annotate or share an annotated version of the poem with students. Highlight new vocabulary or concepts and provide definitions and explanations. You may also include pictures as you annotate. These pictures can be related to the poems or the poets.

Virtual Read-Alouds

Even in distance-learning settings, students benefit from read-alouds. Choose short portions of books to read aloud with your students to provide time for discussion and reflection. During a virtual read-aloud, it is essential that your students can see the text clearly. For synchronous learning, you may show a book to your class by holding it up to your camera or by sharing a digital copy on your screen. You can also record yourself doing a read-aloud and share the video for asynchronous learning. Keep in mind that recorded read-alouds may limit meaningful discussions of the text.

Share the text with students while you read aloud.

Make It Real

Grades PK–K	Grade 1	Grade 2
Provide oral and visual prompts that support fundamental understanding of print.	Challenge students to think deeply about reading aloud as you model it for them.	Encourage students to think about the text and beyond the text as you read to them.

Grades PK–K

- If sharing your screen, highlight the text and/or use the cursor to follow the text as you read.
- Pause to point out details and important words in the images.

Grade 1

- Discuss reading rate, volume, phrasing, and expression as a class.
- Record yourself reading a text with proper and improper rate, volume, phrasing, and expression. Compare the recordings as a class.

Grade 2

- Have students write questions that come to mind as they listen to you read.
- Ask students to discuss connections they made to the text.
- Discuss why the author made the choices they made as they were writing.

More for You

Perfect Fit Read-Aloud video

tcmpub.digital/50/readaloud

Keep in Mind

When choosing books, include diverse authors and a wide range of genres. Read books related to your students' interests, but also cover topics that are new and exciting to students. Bright, engaging artwork and clearly readable text makes for great read-alouds.

Name the Picture

When visuals are used correctly, they increase engagement and help students access background knowledge. Show students a picture related to a topic you are studying. After showing a picture, ask students to name or caption the picture. Students may write or type their responses. The picture you choose should have a primary focus but may have numerous "right" answers. This activity helps students understand the purpose and structure of captions, provides opportunities to build vocabulary, and promotes estimated spelling. Encourage students to also share their own pictures related to a topic. Students can take turns presenting their pictures and writing captions for other pictures.

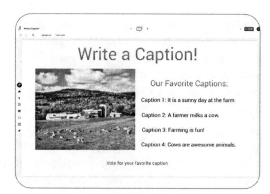

Visual literacy is important for early readers.

Make It Real

Grades PK–K	Grade 1	Grade 2
Discuss the picture with students to access prior knowledge.	Encourage students to be creative with their captions.	Engage students by discussing their captions as a class.
• Ask students to describe the picture and how the picture relates to the topic you have been studying. • Work with students to complete *About the Picture* (page 81) as they study the pictures more thoroughly.	• Have students brainstorm key words that come to mind when they see the picture. • Ask students to include specific vocabulary words in their captions.	• Remind students to be respectful when providing feedback to their peers. • Ask each student to choose their favorite caption and explain why they like it.

More for You

Keep in Mind

Use a search engine to find pictures. Don't forget to check the background and context of the pictures to make sure they are school-appropriate. If teaching synchronously, ask students to write their captions using the chat feature. If teaching asynchronously, have students post their captions through an online board.

Hot and Cold Words

When introducing a topic, use classroom surveys to find out which words students know. Ask students to describe whether related vocabulary words are *hot* or *cold*. Hot words are words students know well. Cold words are words with which they are unfamiliar. If teaching synchronously, students can share their thoughts by chatting directly with you. If working asynchronously, have students post their responses through an online platform or survey. Review students' posts or the survey results so you can see which words your students are already familiar with and which are new to them.

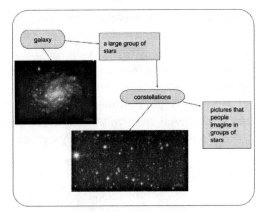

Visually sharing words helps students make connections.

Make It Real

Grades PK–K	Grade 1	Grade 2
Clearly model the activity for younger students. • Give examples of hot words: "*Leaf* is a hot word. I know what it means. A leaf is something I see on a tree." • Give examples of cold words: "*Roots* is a cold word. I'm not sure what it means."	Encourage students to learn about the cold words on their own as well as with you. 1. Have each student create a cold-word vocabulary map. The map should include a definition and pictures. 2. Ask students to share their maps with the class.	Add new dimensions to the activity to challenge students. • Ask students to connect hot and cold words together (visually or through words) to help them remember the words. • Have students complete *Cold Words* (page 82). Then ask them to share their cold words for each unit of study.

More for You

Keep in Mind

Ask students to vote on their top three hot and cold words. Review the results of this formative assessment to make key decisions about how to scaffold appropriately for students.

The Five Senses

Build students' social and emotional learning through mindfulness activities. One helpful activity requires students to focus on their five senses. Begin the activity by asking students to pay attention to their senses for one minute. Then, ask students to walk around for one minute and stop in a new location. Finally, ask students to pay attention to their senses once again. Ask questions, such as: *What do you notice? What feels different? How did your body react to the new location?*

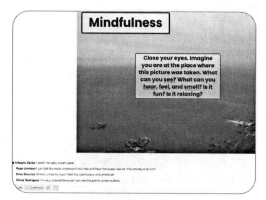

Students post on Seesaw about their five senses.

Make It Real

Grades PK–1	Grades 2–5	Grades 6–12
Modify the activity for younger students.	Use a variety of activities to focus students as they think about their senses.	Add new dimensions to the activity once students are comfortable with the concept of mindfulness.

Grades PK–1

Modify the activity for younger students.

- Focus on one sense at a time, as young students may have difficulty thinking about each of their senses separately. Help them focus by naming each and reminding them what to think about.
- To increase the fun factor, tell students to dance to their new locations. Then, when the time is up, tell them to "Freeze!"

Grades 2–5

Use a variety of activities to focus students as they think about their senses.

- Ask students to tense and relax their muscles before focusing on their senses.
- Have students practice breathing exercises as they quietly connect with the world around them.

Grades 6–12

Add new dimensions to the activity once students are comfortable with the concept of mindfulness.

- Create a space during the day where students can practice their favorite mindfulness activities.
- Allow students to share their favorite mindfulness activities with others and explain why they find the activities helpful.

Keep in Mind

There are countless mindfulness resources online. Search for "mindfulness activities for children" or "mindfulness activities for teens" in the search engine of your choice. Think about compiling your favorite activities on an online platform that your students can access.

Mindfulness Hunts

Create a mindfulness "scavenger hunt" to provide an authentic activity students can complete to experience the benefits of mindfulness. Create a list of activities students can complete during a set amount of time. The complexity of the activities will depend on the ages of your students. Your checklist may include various activities:

- Take ten deep breaths.
- Think of one thing you are grateful for.
- Count the lines on your hand.
- Remember a happy event.
- Do a yoga pose for ten seconds.

Mindfulness Hunt

1. Think of something good that happened to you today.
2. Take 5 deep breaths (breathe in through your nose and out through your mouth).
3. Stand up and stretch your arms above your head for 10 seconds.
4. Shake out your arms and legs for 10 seconds each to get rid of any stress or tension.
5. Think of one thing you are looking forward to this week.

Focusing on mind and body helps students relax.

Make It Real

Grades PK–1

Make sure young students understand the activity and what is expected of them.

- Prior to the scavenger hunt, practice each mindfulness activity as a class.
- Keep students on task with short lists. Include no more than three mindfulness activities in each hunt.

Grades 2–5

Encourage students to talk about their experiences.

- After completing the scavenger hunt, have students share their favorite activities. They can share on *Reflecting on Mindfulness* (page 83).
- Encourage students to share ideas they would like included in future mindfulness hunts.

Grades 6–12

Challenge students to create their own mindfulness scavenger hunts.

- Direct students to mindfulness resources that will help them create their scavenger hunts.
- Encourage students to plan their hunts using *Designing a Mindfulness Hunt* (page 84).

More for You

Keep in Mind

Encourage older students to use photographs and art to enhance the design of their scavenger hunts. If teaching synchronously, choose a student-created hunt to complete as a class by sharing your screen.

Emoji Reactions

Help students identify and connect emotions, from warm and fuzzy feelings (peace and joy) to those that are more uncomfortable (frustration and anger). Read short scenarios or stories that depict different feelings. Provide students with several emoji choices that showcase the feelings they experience as they listen to the text. Then, discuss the emojis that students chose. Allow students to recognize that there are different reactions to the text, showing that not everyone interprets or responds to events in the same way.

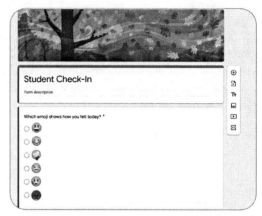

Students describe how they feel using emojis.

Make It Real

Grades PK–1

Younger students may have some trouble responding with virtual emojis.

- Ask each student to draw different faces on paper. Model for students how to hold up their "paper emojis" to their cameras.

- Allow time for students to make their self-drawn faces more detailed to really share their feelings.

Grades 2–7

Create multiple opportunities for students to reflect on their emotions.

- Choose a dynamic text that is likely to elicit several different emotions from students. Pause a few times during the reading to allow students to provide emoji-based feedback.

- Use virtual polls or surveys that record each student's emoji response. Review the poll results as a class.

Grades 8–12

Add new dimensions to the activity to engage older students in meaningful ways.

- Discuss how changes in the scenario would affect their emotional reactions.

- Have students discuss how an emoji or pairing of emojis can convey complex emotions.

Keep in Mind

Before starting this activity, show students how to access emoji reactions on your virtual classroom platform or their own devices. If teaching younger students, you may need to model this multiple times.

Gear Up with Gratitude

Gratitude is a complex emotion. It is the quality of being thankful or grateful. Discuss the meaning of gratitude with your students. Brainstorm examples of gratitude as a class. Help students understand the importance of gratitude by providing moments where they can show their appreciation for positive aspects in their day. Complete student reflections about gratitude on online platforms or in small groups.

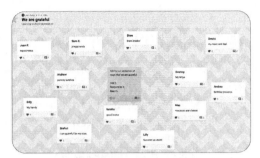

Students list what they are grateful for on Padlet.

Make It Real

Grades PK–1

Clearly model gratitude activities for younger students.

- Tell students three things you are grateful for. Then, brainstorm a list of different things students might be grateful for.

- Help students think about their own feelings as they complete *My Grateful Gears* (page 85).

Grades 2–6

Challenge students to think deeply about their moments of gratitude.

- Brainstorm a list of things students might be grateful for. Ask students to explain the reasoning behind their grateful moments.

- Allow time for students to complete *Gear Up with Gratitude* (page 86) and share their responses in small groups.

Grades 7–12

Use videos to start meaningful classroom discussions about gratitude.

- Locate and share short videos of people expressing gratitude.

- Ask students to make short videos describing their grateful moments. Create an online platform where students can post their videos.

More for You

Keep in Mind

If you create an online board that features student videos, think about starting a new board each week. Otherwise, sharing boards may become overcrowded and difficult to navigate.

Before asking students to create videos, learn about their technology resources. Then, help them locate information about how to create videos using the resources they have.

Virtual Vision Boards

Virtual vision boards are great ways to learn about your students. They also help students learn more about themselves and set goals for the future. Introduce the concept by working on a vision board as a class. Focus the board on that week's learning goals or another topic. Don't be afraid to be silly! Students will be more interested in the activity if you introduce it in a fun way, such as creating a board that details each student's greatest wishes (realistic or otherwise). Once you've created a virtual vision board as a class, allow students to build their own boards.

This sixth grader has big plans!

Make It Real

Grades PK–2	Grades 3–7	Grades 8–12
Younger students may need support to create virtual vision boards. • Have students create physical vision boards with paper and markers before asking them to make virtual ones. • Create virtual boards with students by typing their thoughts on an online platform. Show students their boards and discuss what they created.	Encourage students to be creative when designing their virtual vision boards. • Ask students to include related photos, videos, quotations, and songs in their vision boards. • Within their vision boards, ask students to include step-by-step plans of how they will accomplish their goals.	Give older students more freedom with the activity. • Provide students with multiple prompts to choose from as they create their virtual vision boards. • Challenge students to format their boards in unique and interactive ways by incorporating timelines, flow charts, hyperlinks, and other infographics.

Keep in Mind

Use questions to support students' development of their vision boards:

• What do you look forward to?

• What is something you love and hope to be able to do?

What Do You Think?

When teaching English learners (ELs), use quick formative assessments to check for understanding or progress toward understanding. One formative assessment you can use repeatedly is the simple question: *What do you think?* This question encourages students to summarize and reflect on new content. You can pose questions using interactive online platforms. These platforms allow students to answer questions through text or by recording video responses. Support learners by providing sentence frames and vocabulary banks. These supports will help ensure that all students are able to respond to new content and engage in classroom discussions.

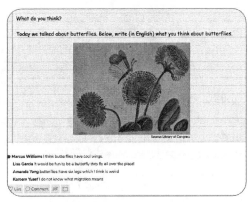

Students respond to their teacher on Seesaw.

Make It Real

Grades PK–1	Grades 2–4	Grades 5–12
Provide encouraging support as students answer questions about new content.	Pose additional questions to help students remember key points about new content.	Support student learning through modeling and the use of visuals.

Grades PK–1

- Address students by name, and provide students with positive feedback to help build their confidence.
- When working with sentence frames, model for students different ways to complete the sentences.

Grades 2–4

- What do you think about the story?
- Who did we learn about?
- What did you learn?
- Who was your favorite character?

Grades 5–12

- If teaching synchronously, pose questions to native English-speaking students first so that their responses may serve as models for ELs.
- Post videos and photos related to new content for students to review on their own time.

Keep in Mind

Review appropriate use of virtual platforms with students. Decide what social media features students are allowed to use in the classroom and which ones may be too distracting.

Patterns in Poetry

Poetry is a great way to engage and support English learners. Poems can be used to reinforce new content, introduce vocabulary, assess reading comprehension, and build oral reading fluency. Short, repetitive poems are especially helpful for ELs. Shorter texts help students build their reading skills with confidence. In addition, repetitive texts reinforce vocabulary and help students think ahead as they read. Find images and videos that relate to poems to help support student understanding.

Repeated words and illustrations help with comprehension.

Make It Real

Grades PK–1	Grades 2–8	Grades 9–12
Provide multiple oral reading opportunities for younger students.	Encourage students to use different media to showcase their understanding of poems.	Ask students to write their own poems about what they are learning in class.
• First, read a poem to students. Then, perform a choral reading as a class.	• Ask students to summarize poems using images or videos or to share songs that remind them of poems they have read.	• Encourage students to use simple poetic structures, such as an ABAB rhyme scheme or haiku. Provide several examples of each poetic structure for students to reference.
• Encourage students to record themselves reading poems. Tell students to record themselves reading poems as many times as they want and share their favorite recordings with you.	• Have students record themselves reading poems. Emphasize that students can record themselves multiple times and then choose the interpretation they like best to share with you.	• Ask students to find photos and videos that capture the spirit of their poems. Then, ask students to caption their photos and videos with lines from their poems.

Keep in Mind

Encourage students to submit "test" recordings before completing their assignments. Their test recordings will let you know if students understand how to use virtual recording platforms or need more guidance.

Chat Features

When teaching synchronously, you will quickly learn the importance of your virtual platform's chat features. You should use these features to engage English learners with new content, encourage classroom discussions, and assess student learning. When posing questions that you want answered through chat features, support learners by sharing related sentence frames and word banks. Also, think about giving students the questions ahead of time. This will help these learners feel more prepared for whole-group discussions.

Chat

From Me to Everyone:
One characteristic of a good president is ____.

From James to Everyone:
trustworthy

From Aubrie to Everyone:
honesty

From Jill to Everyone:
Integrity

From Dani to Everyone:
integrity

Sentence frames allow students to respond more easily.

Make It Real

Grades PK–1	Grades 2–7	Grades 8–12
Support younger students as they become acquainted with chat features.	Give students time to practice chatting in small groups.	Actively scaffold learning throughout your lessons by using the chat feature.
• Explain to students how to use chat features. Set clear expectations and help them become comfortable using the chat. • Ask questions that can be answered by completing simple sentence frames, such as *I like the __. I see the __. I want a __. This is a __.*	• Ask responsible students to lead discussions, reading questions and related sentence frames aloud to the group. • Encourage students to complete sentence frames in as many ways as they can. Then, ask them to share their chat discussions with the rest of the class.	• Ask students to respond to short, clearly written questions in the chat feature as you work through your lesson. Rephrase initial questions orally so learners have chances to respond after viewing other students' responses. • Only after submitting written responses, ask students to begin to submit oral responses as well when called on in class.

Keep in Mind

Most platforms do not allow you to share your screen and show your chat feature so that you can model how to use it for students. However, you can do a screen recording of yourself using the chat feature and share that video with students, if necessary. Be sure to allow plenty of wait time for students to type responses.

Speaking Summaries

Help English learners review new content with assigned summaries. After teaching a lesson, ask students to use the lesson's content objectives to create quick summaries of their learning. Ensure understanding of this task by modeling and completing several summaries with students. Have students record themselves reading their summaries. Encourage students to include divergent thoughts and questions in their summary recordings. These recordings will reinforce new content and build oral reading fluency for learners.

Students are asked to record their responses on Flipgrid.

Make It Real

Grades PK–1	Grades 2–7	Grades 8–12
Simplify summary activities for younger students.	Challenge students to provide longer summaries.	Encourage older students as they work.
• Provide sentence frames, such as *Today we learned three things about ____. The most important thing I learned today was ____.*	• Before having them record themselves, review new vocabulary words with students.	• Have students include questions and wonderings in their summaries.
• Keep summaries short, between one to three sentences in length.	• Provide word banks to support the summary recordings.	• In their summaries, ask students to describe the main ideas and define vocabulary words from the new content.
• Encourage students to practice reading summaries aloud a few times before recording themselves.		

Keep in Mind

Review best practices with students for recording audio. Tell them to make sure that they are speaking loudly and clearly enough for others to understand them. Remind students to avoid "dead air" in their recordings.

Viva Vocabulary

Before introducing new content, consider providing English learners with small-group vocabulary support. Use pictures, videos, and realia to introduce vocabulary. In their small groups, ask students to discuss the words, share representations, write definitions, or use the vocabulary words in sentences. Ask students to describe how the pictures, videos, and realia you have provided relate to the vocabulary words. Then, encourage students to share their own photos and videos that are related to the vocabulary words.

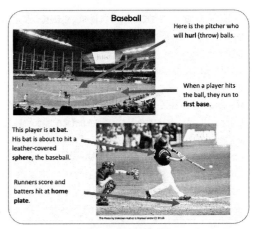

Images help define these vocabulary words.

Make It Real

Grades PK–1

Younger students will likely need more in-depth support with new vocabulary.

- When working in small groups, provide prompts when necessary: *What does that picture show? What do you think this word means?* Use labels to support students as they learn vocabulary words associated with the pictures.

- Help students think more deeply about the words by having them complete *My New Word* (page 87).

Grades 2–6

Encourage students to use new vocabulary in different ways.

- Ask students to write sentences using vocabulary words. Encourage them to record themselves reading their sentences.

- Ask students to use their vocabulary lists to predict what the class's new content may be about. Help them make connections as they begin each new learning unit.

Grades 7–12

Challenge students to write longer pieces featuring the new vocabulary words.

- Ask students to use context clues in their writing to define the vocabulary words. If necessary, model for them how to do this.

- Encourage students to share their writing within small groups.

More for You

Vocabulary Introduction video
tcmpub.digital/50/vivavocab

Keep in Mind

Help students review new words and definitions with virtual flashcards. Then, test their new vocabulary skills using virtual polls. Be sure to always include context when working on new vocabulary words with English learners.

Small-Group Work

While understanding your students' individual skill sets will take some time, working in small groups will provide opportunities for observation and insight. Plan and provide small-group instruction to support student learning. You may choose to schedule small-group time in advance or dedicate parts of whole-class instruction to small groups. Either way, ensure that students understand the expectations to maximize small-group time. Be clear about the timing and the concepts that will be taught. Though the idea of multiple virtual small groups may seem difficult, they can be wildly successful by giving students opportunities for more direct learning as well as social-emotional growth.

High schoolers work well in structured small groups.

Make It Real

Grades PK–2

Students will need support and guidance in small groups.

- Tell students what to expect from small groups, and support students as they get used to working more closely with you and their peers.

- Based on school and district regulations, ask parents or caregivers to supervise small groups so you can run multiple groups at once.

Grades 3–6

Help students navigate small-group work productively.

- Give clear guidelines for small-group sessions if you will not be working directly with students. Have students keep track of their learning using *Small-Group Update* (page 88).

- Provide students concrete tasks or assignments to work on while they're in small groups.

Grades 7–12

Student collaboration promotes social-emotional well-being for teenagers.

- Use small groups to overcome learning gaps, foster discussion, and engage reluctant learners.

- Create groups with diverse student viewpoints.

- Encourage responsible students to take charge and lead small-group work when possible.

More for You

Keep in Mind

When using breakout rooms during live class, visit different rooms to monitor student progress. Make sure students write down the assignment or take a screenshot before going into their breakout rooms. Small-group work can also happen asynchronously using shared documents.

Small-Group Roles

Allow students to be fully engaged in small groups by assigning positions and duties. This will hold students accountable while also providing them with a fun way to showcase their individual skills. In order for groups to be productive, assign roles with each student's strengths and weaknesses in mind. There are countless possible roles, including:

 recorder—student who keeps track of ideas to share with the larger class or teacher

 timekeeper—student who manages time, identifying how much time is left

 encourager—student who encourages participation of all members

 spokesperson—student who shares group ideas with the whole class

Assigning roles helps keep students on track.

Make It Real

Grades PK–3

Every student will want a special title and responsibility.

- Create enough positions that every group member has their own job.
- Invent varied roles to best fit student capabilities.
- Clarify the requirements of each role.

Grades 4–8

Keep students engaged and focused during small groups.

- Prevent students from getting distracted with roles that require active participation.
- Use a rubric to help students identify their success in completing their roles.

Grades 9–12

Assign roles wisely and with purpose.

- Find leaders who will encourage focused and positive interaction during small-group sessions.
- Ask students which roles they want and why. But also keep reluctant learners on their toes by giving them important roles that require their active participation.

More for You

Small-Group Roles video
tcmpub.digital/50/roles

Keep in Mind

Regularly switch small-group roles around to give students chances to try different roles. This will keep them more actively engaged. Also, ask students for suggestions for new roles that might help their groups as they get more comfortable in small-group settings.

Simplify Directions

In a virtual setting, teaching and overseeing small-group work may seem intimidating. But the benefits of working with students in a small-group setting outweigh the deterrents. In small-group settings, students may also feel slightly overwhelmed, especially when the assignment is too complex for them to tackle easily. To help students stay focused and productive, provide small groups with simple, written directions. This will help students to feel comfortable and to take charge of their learning while also giving them structure for their small-group time.

Visual directions may help students stay focused.

Make It Real

Grades PK–2

Students and parents will need very straightforward instructions.

- Keep your language clear and student-focused.

- Use pictures when possible to support the words.

- Consider providing separate adult directions so caregivers can help more effectively.

Grades 3–6

These students need structure and guidance to succeed in small groups.

- Support students by consistently checking on their progress both within their groups and through daily or weekly check-ins.

- Give students an easy way to ask you questions during small-group time.

Grades 7–12

Direct small groups based on students' needs and personalities.

- Provide more detailed instructions for groups that need extra help.

- Encourage all students to participate and to ask questions if they have any.

- Promote positive and respectful collaboration among these teenagers.

Keep in Mind

Sharing directions that are fun and easy to read will help students thrive in small groups. Give instructions through online platforms that break things down in simple ways and are easy for students and parents to access.

What Do You Need?

One of the most challenging aspects of virtual learning is confidently meeting individual student needs. However, small groups give you more direct access to students that could use assistance in certain subjects or topics. Host regularly scheduled small-group sessions where individual students (or groups of students) can identify learning targets they want assistance with. Use the scheduled times to meet small groups, discover issues, and address the identified needs of students. These sessions will help you map student needs and learning gaps while providing students with the additional support they need.

Zoom Group Chat

From Nico to Everyone:
Ms. Jump can you explain long division again.

From Karl to Everyone:
^^me too

From Kamala to Everyone:
I got division but don't understand remainders

From Nico to Everyone:
yeah remainders were hard too

From Me to Everyone:
Great ideas, group! We can definitely cover long division in our group today.

From Stacey to Everyone:
Can we do long division word problems too?

From Acacia to Everyone:
which one is the divisor and which one's the dividend ?

From Kamala to Everyone:
I thought one of them was a quotient

From Me to Everyone:
Got it, let's go!! ✚

Students can help with their own learning.

Make It Real

Grades PK–1

You will need to help younger students realize what subjects they want to focus on.

- Monitor individual student strengths and weaknesses through formative assessments and check-ins during whole-class instruction.
- Ask students who need help in particular areas to assess their needs more deeply and ask them how they feel.
- Communicate with families to further discover student needs.

Grades 2–5

Encourage metacognitive thinking by students so they can self-identify what they need and share with you.

- It may take some time for students to comfortably self-evaluate. Encourage and support them as they learn how to think about their own learning.
- Make groups comfortable and informative for everyone involved. Allow students to share feedback in individual ways, such as on *I Need Help with* ____ (page 89), rather than orally sharing.

Grades 6–12

Help students feel more confident about asking for help.

- Give students ways to privately submit topics that they need support with.
- Remind everyone that getting extra help is not only smart but necessary in a virtual learning environment.
- Schedule one-on-one meetings or groups of two to three (if possible, based on school and district regulations) to provide individualized support.

More for You

Keep in Mind

Use a shared document or chat feature for students to write suggestions for what content to cover during small-group sessions.

Everybody Shares

Sharing knowledge with peers is an essential component of social-emotional learning. Luckily, authentic student conversation about a topic or subject *can* happen virtually. After learning content through videos, reading texts, or teacher-led lectures, provide each small group of students with a shared virtual document. Students can share the information they learned as well as questions they still have. They can also add to other students' ideas and create charts with connections and authentic learning notes.

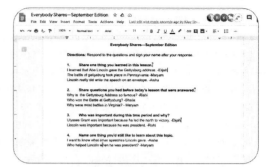

Collaborating online is an effective strategy.

Make It Real

Grades PK–3

Students may need help navigating the technology.

- Demonstrate exactly how to add to the shared virtual document.
- Provide clear expectations for how students can respond to ideas shared by their peers.

Grades 4–6

Get the whole class involved and thinking creatively.

- Have every student share what they learned, as well as respond to two or three peers.
- Showcase special document tools, such as creating a chart or using bold font. Encourage structuring notes using charts or bullet points.

Grades 7–12

Older students should demonstrate a more thorough learning analysis within these shared documents.

- Ask students to make detailed, well-written additions to the shared virtual documents.
- Require each student to respond to all the peers in their small group as well as discuss with those in other groups.
- Prevent surface-level sharing by asking questions and leaving comments that stimulate deep thinking.

More for You

Everybody Shares video
tcmpub.digital/50/shares

Keep in Mind

Use a shared document or online platform for this activity. You can open several shared virtual documents and small groups can rotate and add information to the various sheets.

Virtual Exit Tickets

Check in with students before they "leave" your virtual classroom. Use a prompt to assess student understanding. In a virtual classroom, students will often submit their responses using an online platform. However, students may also showcase their knowledge with oral responses. If teaching synchronously, each student can quickly share their response before they sign out. Adjust your prompt based on the content. For math, students may complete problems that showcase their learning from the lesson. For social studies, students may write lists of things that led to an important event. For language arts, students may describe a main character in three words. These activities should be short, meaningful, and easy to assess.

This is a quick formative assessment about fractions.

Make It Real

Grades PK–1

For younger students, display visuals from the lesson to reinforce new content.

- Use sentence frames and word banks to support student responses.
- Display related images, vocabulary, and key facts that students can refer to as they respond to the exit ticket prompt.

Grades 2–5

Promote further learning by responding to students' exit tickets.

- Ask each student to submit a one-sentence response. Then, highlight responses that answer the prompt accurately.
- Have students record individual answers using an online platform. Then, provide feedback to students to further their learning.

Grades 6–12

Adjust the activity to challenge older students.

- Encourage students to support their written responses with links to related photos, videos, or audio recordings.
- Ask students to discuss other students' responses and describe why they are strong.

Keep in Mind

If students want to support their responses with photos, videos, or audio recordings, provide them with a list of useful websites. If using an online platform, create a lively, visual discussion by encouraging students to respond to their peers with relevant multimedia.

Greatest Takeaways

Zero in on big ideas using this strategy. Provide students with a forum to share their greatest takeaways. Are they on target or off the map? A close eye on their takeaways will indicate whether students are garnering the information needed or if they require additional support. This assessment can be as informal or formal as you like. You may ask students a question at the end of a lesson, such as *After reading the text about Paul Revere, what are your greatest takeaways?* Or, you can encourage more detailed responses to learning, such as *Name five things you learned about Paul Revere's ride.*

Students share their takeaways on Jamboard.

Make It Real

Grades PK–1

Discussing their greatest takeaways may be difficult for young students.

- Simplify the language of the activity. Ask students questions, such as *What did you learn?* or *What was the main idea of the lesson?*

- Model oral and written responses for students. Encourage them to respond using complete sentences, whether they are speaking or writing.

Grades 2–5

Encourage students to explain their thinking.

- Ask students to explain why they think the information they have presented is important.

- Ask students to think of their greatest takeaways as a "main idea" and support their responses with key details.

Grades 6–12

Add new dimensions to the activity to engage students.

- Challenge students to provide two or more takeaways as well as respond to their peers' takeaways.

- Encourage students to summarize their knowledge before providing their greatest takeaways. Have them respond to *The Big Review* (page 90) before sharing their thoughts with others.

More for You

The Big Review
(grades 6–12) 90

Keep in Mind

Add variety to this activity by asking a student to provide their greatest takeaway. Then, ask the rest of the class to provide details on why the student's takeaway is important. If teaching synchronously, ask students to respond using the chat feature. If teaching asynchronously, ask students to respond using an online platform.

Check for Understanding

Are your students getting it? Or do you need to regroup and reteach? In the midst of a great lesson, quick check-ins provide the formative data needed to make instructional decisions. Many virtual platforms provide opportunities for formative assessment. For example, when you need in-the-moment feedback, you can use thumbs-up/thumbs-down or polling features. Use these formative assessments to check for understanding quickly and guide future instruction. Student responses will highlight needs for reteaching, additional support, and targeted feedback.

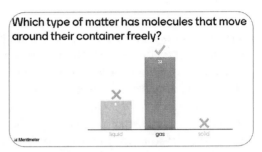

This poll identifies a small group of students who need reteaching.

Make It Real

Grades PK–1	Grades 2–7	Grades 8–12
Clearly model for students what is expected during formative assessments.	Use polling features for quick, detailed feedback.	Ask older students to summarize their learning.

Grades PK–1

Clearly model for students what is expected during formative assessments.

- Show students how to hold their thumbs up to their cameras so that they are seen, or use this feature in their virtual class platform.

- Practice formative assessments throughout the day: *What do we do if we understand? Yes, we put our thumbs up. What do we do if we want more help? We put our thumbs down.*

Grades 2–7

Use polling features for quick, detailed feedback.

- Check for student understanding with multiple-choice questions based on new content.

- Add open-ended questions to your polls so that students may submit their thoughts and questions about new material.

Grades 8–12

Ask older students to summarize their learning.

- Challenge students to write six-word summaries of the lesson through the chat feature. The shortness of the summaries will make it easier for you to read quickly and also challenges students to analyze more deeply.

- Ask students to describe the central idea of new content and defend their opinions with examples from the lesson. Have them share this learning in an online platform so you can quickly see all students' responses.

Keep in Mind

Introduce new technology, such as polling apps, with low-stakes prompts. For example, create a practice poll that asks students to choose their favorite day of the week. Discuss the results as a class to show students how the technology may be used in the future. Then, begin using the technology for true formative assessments.

The Power of Voice

Instead of asking for written responses to prompts, change things up! Ask students to respond with audio recordings. Within their recordings, students can share thoughts and questions that are related to the prompts. In many audio recording platforms, students are able to engage and interact with one another, creating lively classroom debates and discussions. No matter their grade level, help students plan their audio recordings before recording themselves. Teach them to draft scripts and think about how to use intonation, volume, and pace with their voices.

Many cell phones have easy-to-use recording apps.

Make It Real

Grades PK–1	Grades 2–7	Grades 8–12
Support young students as they create audio recordings.	Encourage students to be creative with their audio recordings.	Use audio recordings to launch engaging classroom discussions.
• Provide clear instructions and model the use of simple recording platforms. • Tell students to keep their oral responses short—one to two sentences in length. • Accept unrecorded oral responses when necessary.	• Tell students their responses may include quotations from books, movies, or songs that support their thinking. • Allow students to create "second takes" on prompts by interviewing fellow students or family members.	• Ask students to create two audio recordings, one that asks a question related to new content and another that answers a fellow student's recorded question. • Have students discuss the questions and answers and how these interactions furthered their thinking.

Keep in Mind

Remind students that their audio clips should not have much dead air. They should speak clearly and fluently. Model correct speaking pace and volume for your students. Think about creating a list of best practices for recording audio that you can share with your class.

Drag and Drop

Use drag-and-drop activities to discover what connections students are making with new content. Drag-and-drop activities can be created on a variety of online platforms. Based on the content, they can be as simple or complex as you need. Here are a few examples of how you can use these activities:

- labeling science diagrams
- defining vocabulary
- sorting words, pictures, and ideas
- ordering events

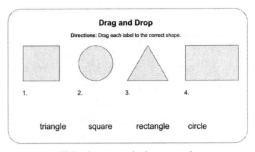

This drag-and-drop math activity is easy to assess.

Make It Real

Grades PK–1	Grades 2–6	Grades 7–12
For young students, keep activities simple.	Use drag-and-drop activities to address appropriate standards.	Challenge students to create their own drag-and-drop activities related to the content.
• Ask students to match pictures with short captions. • Ask students to "build" words using virtual letter tiles. • When creating a question, provide no more than three possible answers.	• Ask students to match causes with their correct effects, place events in the correct order, or sequence steps correctly. • Another option is to have students read a text and then choose details that support the main idea.	• Encourage them to add appropriate gifs and memes to make the learning engaging for their peers. • Choose several student-created activities to complete as a class.

Keep in Mind

Think about creating a variety of drag-and-drop templates that you can reuse throughout the year for different content. Provide these templates to older students when they are creating their own activities.

60-Second Podcasts

The virtual learning process requires the entire classroom community to be on the same page. This includes administrators, teachers, students, and families or caregivers. Prevent families from getting overwhelmed by sharing key information in a concise way. Post a regularly scheduled 60-second podcast with brief, clear updates. Share information about scheduling, pertinent at-home work, and strategies for motivating students. Podcasts could be daily or weekly. The key is to make your podcasts consistent, simple, and easy to follow.

Podcasts are an effective way to communicate.

Make It Real

Grades PK–2	Grades 3–5	Grades 6–12
Give families direct guidance for helping their students stay engaged and organized.	Caregivers may need to help students as they complete independent work.	Families of older students will demonstrate varying levels of involvement.
• Conclude each podcast with an engagement tip. • Dedicate parts of your podcasts to explaining the technology students will be using. • Clarify all schedule changes so parents can make the necessary arrangements.	• Specify when certain at-home assignments are due. • Give suggestions for how families can help their students tackle more complex assignments. • Detail your classroom schedule so parents and caregivers know when they may need to provide additional support.	• Discuss your basic lesson plans and materials. • Help caregivers support students who struggle to stay motivated during independent learning. • Ask parents to hold their students accountable for completing at-home work and paying attention during synchronous instruction.

Keep in Mind

You can make podcasts with free sites or simply record a voice memo and post it to your virtual classroom. Make sure your messages are clear, concise, and shared often.

Family Demonstrations

Parents and other caregivers want to feel involved and provide support as their students learn at home. One way to foster this is to post demonstrations of key work activities for families to observe so they know what their students are engaged in. Show the materials needed, the steps to take, and any common trouble spots. Model student work to indicate what families can expect. For example, share completion of a real-world math problem or literary analysis. These quick demonstrations will help caregivers feel involved and allow them to support students during independent learning.

This father is helping his child complete classwork.

Make It Real

Grades PK–2	Grades 3–6	Grades 7–12
Younger students will need support to complete most of their work.	Parents will primarily use your demonstrations to help students when they get stuck.	Some families don't have the background knowledge to help students with their schoolwork at this level, but you can still help them be involved.
• Make your demonstrations as detailed and adult-focused as possible. • Give easy access to demonstrations on multiple topics. • Use clear, non-academic language in your videos.	• Focus your demonstration on problem spots and harder-to-understand concepts. • Include multiple strategies for completing work so students can choose which one works best.	• Use demonstrations to showcase various virtual teaching techniques. • Ask families to provide emotional support while students complete independent and asynchronous work.

Keep in Mind

You may use your virtual classroom platform to post videos. You can also use a separate app or website reserved solely for your demonstrations.

Two-Way Street

Facilitating an environment where families feel comfortable sharing their questions and concerns with virtual instruction will set students up for success. Questions are inevitable. Set up a forum to share important information in one easy place. Include a place for parents or other caregivers to regularly communicate questions and concerns to you. You may also want to post an FAQ document for families. Having a classroom public forum or document allows everyone to easily find pertinent information and prevents redundancy.

A teacher communicates with a parent via Seesaw.

Make It Real

Grades PK–3

Parents want to ensure that their children are getting the proper help and attention.

- Point out specific times when the subject matter or learning style meets individual student needs.
- Remind families that important classroom practices can and will be implemented virtually.

Grades 4–8

Keeping students engaged and focused will be a key point for these families.

- Provide broad advice on how to encourage student productivity.
- Offer specific strategies designed to excite and motivate students during independent learning.

Grades 9–12

Many families will have questions on how to motivate reluctant learners.

- Explain the best way to structure independent learning time.
- Encourage families to be patient and persistent with their teenage students.
- Offer general tips as well as specific tools to guide students toward success.

Keep in Mind

Use an online platform to set up your FAQ forum or document. Be sure to answer any questions about specific students in a private setting.

Family Nights

Normally, students have chances to introduce you to their parents or other caregivers, whether it's at a holiday party, a lunchtime picnic, or back-to-school night. In a virtual world, these events may not happen or may look very different from normal. Instead, host casual virtual family nights. Allow families to join for read-alouds, games, or celebrations. Theme the family nights to promote fun and connections. Be creative with your themes to keep students and families invested!

Kahoot! quizzes are perfect for family nights!

Make It Real

Grades PK–2	Grades 3–5	Grades 6–12
Plan a special event to engage and excite younger students.	Connect family nights to the classroom in interesting ways.	These parents will enjoy spending time with their teenagers.
• Host a virtual Pizza Party where families can eat pizza (or their other favorite foods) while playing games. • Thrill students with Jammie Jams Night. Families can wear pajamas and listen to a special playlist of music.	• Play games where families can answer trivia questions together. • Have students read play scripts or book passages where each student has an assigned character and unmutes to speak.	• Have students plan the family nights so they have buy-in and want to attend. • Entice students to join with trivia games or competitive tournaments.

Keep in Mind

Family nights do not have to be long. A 15- to 30-minute activity will engage families and build relationships. There are several free websites where you can create games or trivia quizzes. Also, every student has a different family dynamic, so be broad and inclusive with your definition of family night.

Fill-in-the-Blank Fairs

Science fairs, art fairs, language fairs, oh my! As students complete units of study, invite families to join the class in virtual learning fairs. These could be science fairs where students show off their science learning or language fairs where students highlight their new letter-sound knowledge. By allowing students to share their work with families and peers, you will create a wholistic classroom environment that parents can play an active part in.

4TH GRADE ART FAIR

Art fairs are a beautiful way to celebrate.

Make It Real

Grades PK–3	Grades 4–7	Grades 8–12
Students will be eager to share, so encourage families to provide them with structure.	Families can help students improve upon their work.	Encourage student and parent participation.
• Ask parents to help their students practice presenting. • Remind parents to keep track of time as students showcase their work.	• Challenge parents to ask their children deep, meaningful questions about their work. • Provide parents with the fair guidelines as well as suggestions for how students can think outside the box.	• Provide time for students to work collaboratively in preparation for the event. • Encourage students to respond to one another's work. • Brainstorm with students how to create work that is interesting and exciting to share with others.

Keep in Mind

Students can share using several platforms, but be sure to give parents easy access so families can appreciate work after the fair is over.

Appendices Table of Contents

Bibliography

These resources were referenced in the writing of this book.

Benner, Diana. "Digital Icebreakers that Shatter." TCEA. Accessed September 2020. tcea.org/documents/ebooks/TCEA-eBook-Icebreakers-That-Shatter.pdf.

Collaborative for Academic, Social, and Emotional Learning. "Core SEL Competencies." CASEL. Accessed September 2020. casel.org/core-competencies/.

Fleming, Nora. "Why Are Some Kids Thriving During Remote Learning?" Edutopia. Updated April 24, 2020. www.edutopia.org/article/why-are-some-kids-thriving-during-remote-learning.

Frost, Alexandra. "9 Virtual Teaching Success Stories We Can All Learn From." We Are Teachers. Updated May 20, 2020. www.weareteachers.com/virtual-teaching-success-stories/.

Gonzalez, Jennifer. "Creating Moments of Genuine Connection Online." Cult of Pedagogy. Updated August 16, 2020. www.cultofpedagogy.com/genuine-connection-online/.

Hay, Marya. "Distance Learning with Intention and Purpose." Achieve the Core. Updated May 11, 2020. achievethecore.org/aligned/distance-learning-intention-purpose/.

Hollie, Sharroky. The Center for Culturally Responsive Teaching and Learning. Accessed September 2020. www.culturallyresponsive.org.

Johnson, Bethany Lockhart. "Amplifying Student Voices During Distance Learning." Achieve the Core. Updated July 17, 2020. achievethecore.org/aligned/amplifying-student-voices-distance-learning/.

Mora-Flores, Eugenia. *Integrated English Language Development.* Huntington Beach: Shell Education, 2018.

Newman, Jamila. "For Many Schools, It's Back to Distance Learning. Let's Make It Better." *TNTP Blog.* Updated August 11, 2020. tntp.org/blog/post/for-many-schools-its-back-to-distance-learning-lets-make-it-better.

Nguyen, Brad. "What Makes a Good Instructional Video?" Teach. Think. Blog. Updated August 8, 2020. teachthinkblog.wordpress.com/2020/08/08/what-makes-a-good-instructional-video/.

Rice, Kerry, and Kristin Kipp. "How Can Educators Tap Into Research to Increase Engagement During Remote Learning?" EdSurge. Updated May 6, 2020. www.edsurge.com/news/2020-05-06-how-can-educators-tap-into-research-to-increase-engagement-during-remote-learning.

Ralph, Michael. "Teaching Strategies of Award-Winning Online Instructors." Edutopia. Updated April 17, 2020. www.edutopia.org/article/teaching-strategies-award-winning-online-instructors.

Schwartz, Sarah. "What Should We Teach? 5 Steps Keeping Kids on Track This Fall." EdWeek. Updated August 5, 2020. www.edweek.org/ew/articles/2020/08/06/what-should-we-teach-5-steps-for.html.

Tucker, Catlin. "A Flipped Learning Flow for Blended or Online Classes." Updated July 24, 2020. catlintucker.com/2020/07/flipped-learning-flow-for-blended-or-online/.

WBT Systems. "9 Ways to Increase Online Student Engagement." Accessed September 2020. www.wbtsystems.com/learning-hub/blogs/9-ways-to-increase-online-student-engagement.

Westman, Lisa. "Why We Need Differentiation Now More Than Ever." *ASCD Education Update Newsletter,* Vol. 62, No. 5 (May 2020). www.ascd.org/publications/newsletters/education-update/may20/vol62/num05/Why-We-Need-Differentiation-Now-More-Than-Ever.aspx.

Celebration Time!

Directions: On the left side, give a reason to celebrate. On the right side, explain how you think the class should celebrate virtually.

Reason to Celebrate	How to Celebrate Virtually

My Playlist

Directions: List five songs for your class playlist. Tell why you chose each song.

Song 1: _____

Why? _____

_____

Song 2: _____

Why? _____

_____

Song 3: _____

Why? _____

_____

Song 4: _____

Why? _____

_____

Song 5: _____

Why? _____

Name ______________________________ Date ________________ For use with page 22.

Playlist Ideas

Directions: Choose a time of the school day. Pick five songs for your playlist. Tell why you chose each song and how it fits your chosen time of day.

Time of Day: ____________________________

Song 1: ____

Why? ____

____

Song 2: ____

Why? ____

____

Song 3: ____

Why? ____

____

Song 4: ____

Why? ____

____

Song 5: ____

Why? ____

____

_____'s Identity Map

Directions: Draw an identity map for someone else. It can be a real person or a fictional character.

Directions: Compare and contrast your own identity map to the one you created here.

_____

_____

_____

My Captions

Directions: Draw a funny picture. Then, ask a friend to write a funny caption to match the picture.

_____

_____

My Survey

Directions: Write three survey questions. Make them fun and interesting!

Question 1: _____

Question 2: _____

Question 3: _____

Directions: Ask three classmates your questions. Write their answers in the chart.

	_____'s answers	_____'s answers	_____'s answers
Question 1			
Question 2			
Question 3			

Bonus: Make a graph or chart that shows your data.

Social Contract Brainstorm

Directions: Think about the rules and expectations you would like to include in our classroom contract.

1. What is a rule that will help students listen to one another?

   _____

   _____

   _____

   _____

2. What rules or expectations will help students focus on learning?

   _____

   _____

   _____

   _____

   _____

3. Describe other rules and expectations that you think our class should have in our virtual setting.

   _____

   _____

   _____

   _____

   _____

Virtual Greeting Proposal

Directions: Think about how you can make students feel welcome in your class. Share your ideas with your teacher.

1. Describe a virtual greeting we should include in our class.

    _____

    _____

    _____

    _____

2. Why do you think the class should use your greeting?

    _____

    _____

    _____

3. What do you want to call your virtual greeting?

    _____

126453—50 Strategies for Your Virtual Classroom   © Shell Education

Attention Getter Proposal

Directions: Help your teacher determine attention getters that will work with your class.

1. How can your teacher effectively get the attention of students throughout the learning day?

   _____

   _____

   _____

   _____

   _____

2. Why do you think students will respond well to this attention getter?

   _____

   _____

   _____

3. What would you like to name your attention getter?

   _____

For use with
page 34.

Give Me a Break

Directions: A brain break is a fun activity that gives you a break from schoolwork. Brainstorm ideas for brain breaks that you would enjoy. Then, write the directions for your favorite brain break.

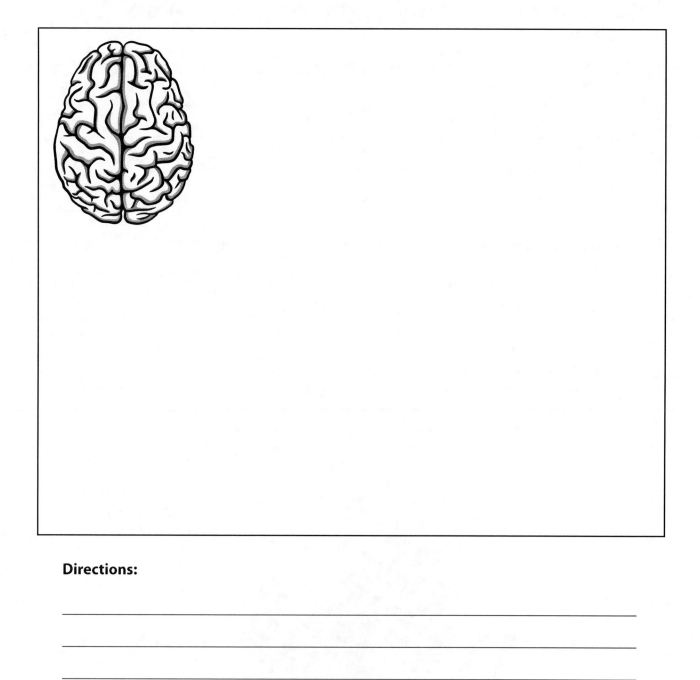

Directions:

_____

_____

_____

_____

_____

126453—50 Strategies for Your Virtual Classroom   © Shell Education

Mystery Word

Directions: Think about the mystery word. Complete these sentences.

1. Today the word was _____

    _

    _____ .

2. The word rhymes with _____

    _

    _____ .

3. The word means _____

    _

    _____

    _

    _____ .

Write It!
Write the mystery word in a sentence.
_____

_ _ _ _ _ _ _ _ _ _ _ _ _ _ _ _ _ _ _ _

_____

_ _ _ _ _ _ _ _ _ _ _ _ _ _ _ _ _ _ _ _

_____

Guess My Word

Directions: Choose a word. The word should follow the phonics rule you have been practicing. Complete these sentences. Write more clues for your word.

Clue 1: I am thinking of a _____ word.

(write phonics rule)

Clue 2: My word rhymes with these words:

_____

_____

Clue 3: _____

_____

_____

Clue 4: _____

_____

_____

Clue 5: The definition of my word is:

_____

_____

_____

About the Picture

Directions: Think about the picture. Then, answer
the questions.

1. What colors do you see? _____

    _____

    _____

2. What does the picture show? _____

    _____

    _____

3. What else do you see? _____

    _____

    _____

4. What would you name the picture? _____

    _____

Name ______________________ Date ______________________

For use with page 41.

Cold Words

Directions: Choose three cold words. Write the definition of each word. Then, write each word in a sentence.

Cold Word 1: ______________________

Definition: ______________________

____

Sentence: ______________________

____

Cold Word 2: ______________________

Definition: ______________________

____

Sentence: ______________________

____

Cold Word 3: ______________________

Definition: ______________________

____

Sentence: ______________________

____

Reflecting on Mindfulness

Directions: Think about the mindfulness hunt.

1. Which activities did you do today?

   _____

   _____

2. What did you learn from the activities?

   _____

   _____

   _____

3. Which activity was your favorite? Why?

   _____

   _____

   _____

4. When might you use these activities in the future?

   _____

   _____

Designing a Mindfulness Hunt

Directions: Design your own mindfulness scavenger hunt.

1. How many activities would you like to include on your hunt? _____

2. What resources have you used to find good mindfulness activities?

   _____

   _____

3. Describe a mindfulness activity that focuses on breathing.

   _____

   _____

   _____

4. Describe a mindfulness activity that focuses on one of the five senses.

   _____

   _____

   _____

5. Describe a mindfulness activity that focuses on memory.

   _____

   _____

   _____

6. What other mindfulness activities would you like to include in your scavenger hunt?

   _____

   _____

   _____

My Grateful Gears

Directions: Think about what you are grateful for. Write your ideas on the gears.

I am grateful for ...

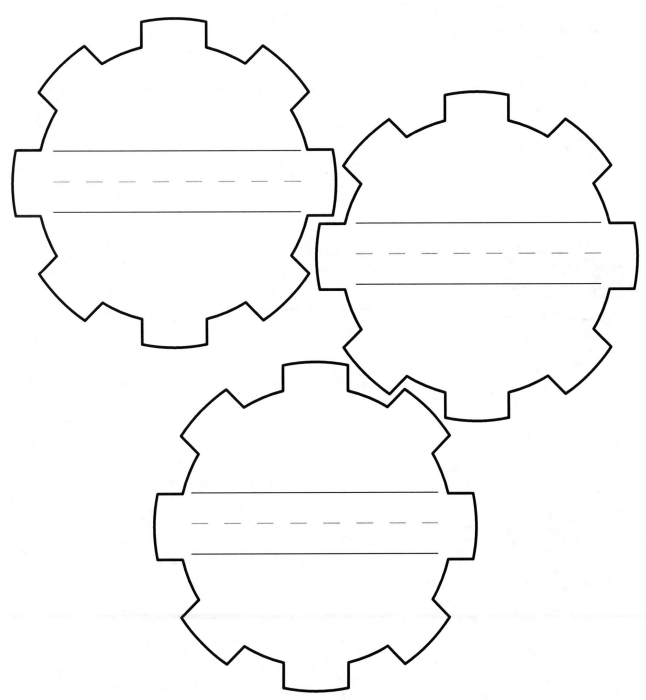

Name ______________________ Date ____________________

For use with page 45.

Gear Up with Gratitude

Directions: Think about gratitude and moments in your life when you've been grateful. Then, answer the questions.

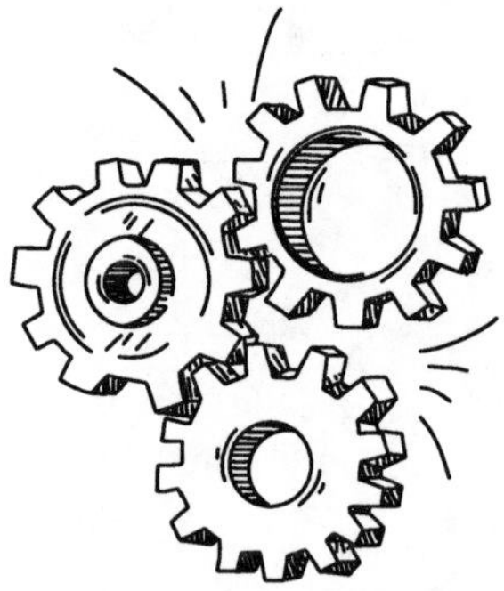

Describe a time when you have felt grateful.

____

____

____

____

____

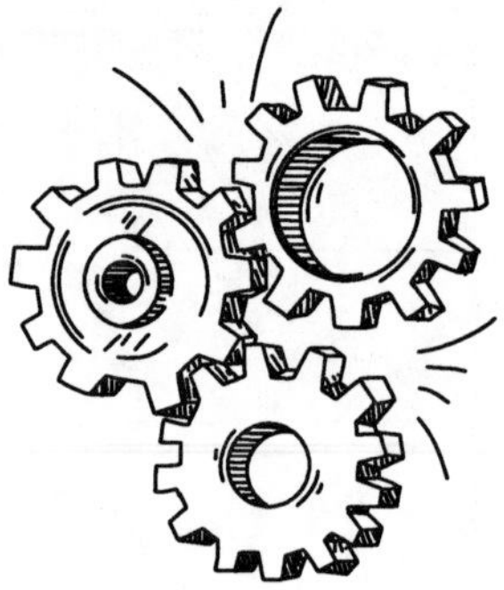

Who do you feel grateful for at school? Why?

____

____

____

____

____

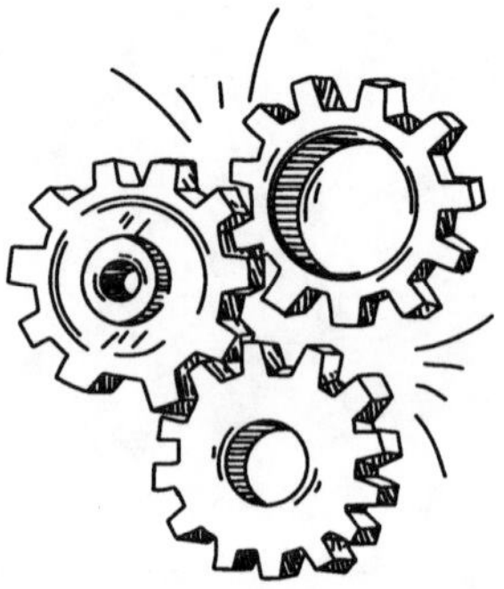

Who do you feel grateful for at home? Why?

____

____

____

____

____

For use with
page 51.

My New Word

Directions: Choose a word. Think about your word.

Write your word.

Draw a picture of your word.

Write your word in a sentence.

Write your word again.

Small-Group Update

Directions: In small groups, your classmates and teacher will say things that help you learn. Fill in the chart during small-group work. Then, write what you learned.

Who said it?	What did they say?	What does this teach me?

_____

_____

_____

_____

_____

I Need Help with _____

Directions: Read the words. Circle what you are good at doing.
Draw squares around what you need more help to do.

physical activity

being polite

music

ART

reading

listening

social studies

SCIENCE

WRITING

speaking

math

computer work

Directions: Decide what you need the most help with. Then, write a
question for your teacher.

_____

_____

_____

_____

The Big Review

Directions: Think about the new content you have studied in class.

1. Write a short summary of what you have learned.

   _____

   _____

   _____

   _____

   _____

2. What were your two greatest takeaways from the lesson? Why did these stand out as important to you?

   _____

   _____

   _____

   _____

   _____

   _____

3. What questions do you still have about the content?

   _____

   _____

   _____

Technology Connections

This chart includes specific app or website suggestions for relevant strategies. The assumption is that most virtual teaching will take place in a Zoom, Google Meet, Microsoft Teams, or WebEx setting. Therefore, those apps are not included in this chart.

When you're deciding which apps or websites to use, start small. Use a couple repeatedly until students and families are comfortable with them. This is especially important in secondary classes where students have multiple teachers assigning work in different apps and websites.

Page	Strategy	Suggested Apps or Websites
17	**Organizing: At-Home Classroom**	document camera
18	**Organizing: Introduction Videos**	Flipgrid, YouTube
19	**Organizing: Home Norms**	Google Docs, Microsoft Word
21	**Organizing: Weekly & Daily Schedules**	Google Docs, Microsoft Word
22	**Building Community: Creating Playlists**	Apple Music, Amazon Music, Spotify, YouTube
23	**Building Community: Identity Maps**	Google Docs, Google Slides, Jamboard, Microsoft PowerPoint, Microsoft Word
24	**Building Community: Caption This!**	Bing!, Google, Yahoo! Search, Jamboard, Padlet
25	**Building Community: Show-and-Tell**	Flipgrid, Jamboard, Padlet
26	**Building Community: Classroom Surveys**	Google Docs, Google Forms
27	**Managing: Social Contracts**	Google Docs, Google Forms, Jamboard, Padlet
28	**Managing: Virtual Greetings**	Flipgrid, Jamboard, Padlet
29	**Managing: Attention Getters**	Flipgrid, Jamboard, Padlet, YouTube
30	**Managing: Bell Ringers**	Flipgrid, Jamboard, Padlet
31	**Managing: Virtual Games**	Flipgrid, Kahoot!
32	**Engaging Students: Scavenger Hunts**	Flipgrid
34	**Engaging Students: Brain Breaks**	Bing!, Google, Yahoo! Search
35	**Engaging Students: "I Wonder" Boards**	Jamboard, Padlet
36	**Engaging Students: Think-Pair-Share**	Google Docs, Microsoft Word
37	**Teaching PK–2 Reading: Phonics Quick Draw**	Bing!, Google, Yahoo! Search, Jamboard, Padlet
38	**Teaching PK–2 Reading: Pick a Poem**	Easy Voice Recorder, Vocaroo, Voice Memos
39	**Teaching PK–2 Reading: Virtual Read-Alouds**	Easy Voice Recorder, Vocaroo, Voice Memos
40	**Teaching PK–2 Reading: Name the Picture**	Bing!, Google, Yahoo! Search, Jamboard, Padlet
41	**Teaching PK–2 Reading: Hot and Cold Words**	Google Docs, Google Forms
42	**Focusing on SEL: The Five Senses**	Jamboard, Headspace.com, Waterford.org

Technology Connections (cont.)

Page	Strategy	Suggested Apps or Websites
43	**Focusing on SEL: Mindfulness Hunts**	Canva, Google Slides, Jamboard, Microsoft PowerPoint, Padlet
44	**Focusing on SEL: Emoji Reactions**	Google Forms, Jamboard, Typeform
45	**Focusing on SEL: Gear up with Gratitude**	iMovie, Magisto, Padlet, Windows Movie Maker, Wondershare FilmoraGo, YouTube
46	**Focusing on SEL: Virtual Vision Boards**	Canva, Google Slides, Jamboard, Microsoft PowerPoint, Padlet, YouTube
47	**Supporting ELs: What Do You Think?**	Flipgrid, Jamboard, Padlet, Seesaw
48	**Supporting ELs: Patterns in Poetry**	Easy Voice Recorder, Flipgrid, Vocaroo, Voice Memos
49	**Supporting ELs: Chat Features**	Flipgrid, Jamboard
50	**Supporting ELs: Speaking Summaries**	Easy Voice Recorder, Flipgrid, Vocaroo, Voice Memos
51	**Supporting ELs: *Viva* Vocabulary**	Flipgrid, Jamboard, Quizlet, Tinycards, Typeform
52	**Using Small Groups: Small-Group Work**	Google Docs, Jamboard
54	**Using Small Groups: Simplify Directions**	Google Slides, Jamboard, Microsoft PowerPoint
55	**Using Small Groups: What Do You Need?**	Google Docs, Jamboard, Microsoft Word
56	**Using Small Groups: Everybody Shares**	Google Docs, Jamboard, Microsoft Word
57	**Monitoring Progress: Virtual Exit Tickets**	Britannica, Google Docs, Google Slides, Jamboard, Microsoft PowerPoint, YouTube
58	**Monitoring: Greatest Takeaways**	Canva, Google Slides, Jamboard, Microsoft PowerPoint, Padlet
59	**Monitoring Progress: Check for Understanding**	Google Forms, Jamboard, Typeform
60	**Monitoring Progress: The Power of Voice**	Easy Voice Recorder, Vocaroo, Voice Memos
61	**Monitoring Progress: Drag and Drop**	Google Slides, Jamboard, Microsoft PowerPoint
62	**Engaging Parents: 60-Second Podcasts**	Anchor, Podbean, Voice Memos, YouTube
63	**Engaging Parents: Family Demonstrations**	Flipgrid, YouTube
64	**Engaging Parents: Two-Way Street**	Seesaw
65	**Engaging Parents: Family Nights**	Kahoot!, Quizlet Live
66	**Engaging Parents: Fill-in-the-Blank Fairs**	Google Docs, Google Slides, Jamboard, Microsoft PowerPoint, Microsoft Word

Useful Applications and Websites

The information provided in this table is intended to briefly introduce you to these digital applications and websites. Most of these resources provide free access for teachers and students, but you'll want to check with your school or district about guidelines for using these programs in your classroom.

Application or Website	Purpose	Examples
A Web Whiteboard awwapp.com/info/	online whiteboard that can be used for modeling and collaboration during synchronous lessons	• solve math problems live with students • brainstorm with students
Canva canva.com	design platform with user-friendly templates to help students and teachers create visual products	• have students create book covers as book reports • ask students to design travel brochures for famous locations in history
Edpuzzle edpuzzle.com	platform for editing or creating interactive video lessons with narration and evaluative tools	• edit videos with questions for students to respond to online • create a video of yourself reading a book and stop to ask questions about the story
Explain Everything explaineverything.com	online whiteboard that can be used for synchronous or recorded asynchronous lessons	• use live to write or draw with students as you teach • create recordings for students to reference when working independently
Flipgrid info.flipgrid.com	online platform where teachers share content and students interact with it through videos, photos, text, emojis, and more	• have students create and share introduction videos • have students respond to prompts and interact with one another
Flippity flippity.net	program that converts Google Sheets into interactive cards and games	• create flashcards for review of previously learned material • use templates to create puzzles and games for important vocabulary words
Google Classroom Question Feature classroom.google.com	aspect of Google Classroom that allows for quick creation and posting of questions; student responses gathered in one location	• write and share survey questions or weekly check-ins • create formative assessments and exit tickets
Google Docs, **Google Sheets**, and **Google Slides** docs.google.com sheets.google.com slides.google.com	applications that allow for live collaboration, including document creation and editing	• collaborate on writing assignments • create, collaborate, and share spreadsheets and presentations

Useful Applications and Websites (cont.)

Application or Website	Purpose	Examples
Google Drawings drawings.google.com	drawing application that allows for live collaboration and document creation	• have students collaborate on drawings during asynchronous learning • ask students to draw responses to literature while watching author videos
Google Forms forms.google.com	survey application that allows for quick creation of surveys and easy collection of results	• create and share summative or formative assessments • implement status surveys of students and families
Google Jamboard jamboard.google.com	online sharing platform and whiteboard for use in synchronous or asynchronous learning	• brainstorm questions about a topic before a unit of study • model the use of shared Google Drive files using the apps for this website
Google Meet meet.google.com	video-communication service available for synchronous class sessions	• conduct whole-class sessions • hold small-group lessons or collaborative meetings
Kahoot! kahoot.com	platform that allows the creation and playing of learning games and quizzes	• conduct formative assessments • increase student activity during synchronous lessons
Loop loophq.io	survey platform that allows interaction between individual students and teachers	• communicate with students to support understanding • give daily exit tickets to assess student learning
Mentimeter mentimeter.com	application designed to get real-time input from students	• create live word clouds on topics of study • conduct polls as formative assessments
Microsoft Teams microsoft.com	communication service with meeting, call, chat, and collaboration features available for synchronous class sessions	• hold whole-class sessions • conduct small-group lessons or collaborative meetings
Nearpod nearpod.com	platform that allows the creation of interactive lessons and provides educational videos on many topics; also allows for creation of videos using presentation software	• convert Microsoft PowerPoint presentations into videos for asynchronous learning • assign interactive videos for asynchronous learning assignments
Padlet padlet.com	online sharing platform and whiteboard for use in synchronous or asynchronous learning	• create collaborative timelines • build class dictionary/thesaurus with important words for the content areas

Useful Applications and Websites (cont.)

Application or Website	Purpose	Examples
Pear Deck peardeck.com	platform that integrates with Google and Microsoft documents to add interactivity and online learning tools	• build interactive lessons for students to use during independent learning • interact with students and assess student learning
Quizizz quizizz.com	platform that allows the creation of quizzes and use of quizzes created by others	• create and share formative assessments • increase student activity during synchronous lessons
Seesaw web.seesaw.me	online platform intended to provide resources and increase interaction for students, teachers, and families	• communicate about at-home learning work and provide individual feedback • have students create products to share what they've learned about a topic of study
Socrative socrative.com	platform that allows the creation of quizzes, exit tickets, and quick questions	• conduct formative and summative assessments • share and assess exit tickets
WebEx webex.com	video-communication service available for synchronous class sessions	• conduct whole-class sessions • hold small-group lessons or collaborative meetings
Whiteboard.fi whiteboard.fi	online whiteboard that can be used for synchronous lessons	• solve math problems live with students • model sentence structure and vocabulary activities with students
Wordle wordle.net/create	program for creating word clouds asynchronously	• create introductory visuals for new units of study • have students export and share what they know about a topic visually
YouTube youtube.com	online platform for viewing and sharing videos	• create a class space to post videos • view videos during asynchronous instruction
Zoom zoom.us	video-communication service available for synchronous class sessions	• conduct whole-class sessions • hold small-group lessons or collaborative meetings

Digital Resources

To support the strategies throughout this book, there are Digital Resources provided in a few different ways.

Fillable PDFs

A fillable PDF of each student activity sheet (pages 69–90) can be downloaded by following these steps:

1. Go to **www.tcmpub.com/digital**.

2. Enter the ISBN, which is located on the back cover of the book, into the appropriate field on the website.

3. Respond to the prompts using this book to view your account and the available digital content.

4. Choose the digital resources you would like to download. You can download all the files at once, or you can download a specific group of files.

Google Docs

Connect here to get a Google Docs copy of the student activities (pages 69–90). Go to **tcmpub.digital/50/google**.

Supporting Videos

Ten of the strategies in this resource have supporting videos that demonstrate the strategies or give further information. To access these videos, visit the short URL links or connect via the QR codes provided on the strategy pages.